the *Cross* and the *Sword*

The Rebellion & Revolution in Chiapas, Mexico

the Cross and the Sword

The Rebellion & Revolution in Chiapas, Mexico

Carl Lawrence
Gold Medallion author of "The Church in China"
with Benjamin Rule

SHANNON
PUBLISHERS

The Cross and the Sword
The Rebellion and Revolution in Chiapas, Mexico
© 1999 by Carl Lawrence and Benjamin Rule

Published by Shannon Publishers
PO Box 575
Artesia, California 90702

Shann Publ@aol.com

Printed in the United States of America

International Standard Book Number: 0-9638575-1-7

Scripture quotations in this publication are from the
New King James Version, Thomas Nelson, Inc.

CONTENTS

———— ✳ ————

A word from the publisher:

This book may sound anti-Catholic at times. That is neither our intent nor our purpose. The Catholic Church of Mexico in general, and in Chiapas specifically, are quite different.

There are five major types of Catholics in Chiapas:

1. Christopagans, the largest group, who have absorbed through syncretism many of the false religions that were in Mexico when Cortez arrived.

2. Catholics who rally under the banner of Liberation Theology.

3. Traditionalists, who want to go back to pre-Pope John XXIII, including the Latin mass.

4. Evangelical Catholics, who have accepted Jesus Christ as the Savior and Lord of their lives, and remain in the Roman Catholic Church as "salt and light."

5. Charismatic Catholics, who believe in the exercise of all the gifts of the Spirit, and are more physically active in their worship than any of the other groups.

As with the Protestant Church in America, there are those that are born, married, and buried in the Church and are Catholics as long as it does not interfere with their everyday lives.

It should be noted that some of the most intense criticism of the Catholic Church comes from the Catholics themselves.

We ask that you read the book, and then make up your own mind about the Church's role in Mexico today.

The nations...served their idols
...even sacrificed their sons and daughters
to the demons, and shed innocent blood,
the blood of the sons and daughters
whom they sacrificed to the idols...
and the land was polluted with the blood.

Psalm 106: 36 - 38

INTRODUCTION

The history of Chiapas, Mexico, is a microcosm of all of mankind living separated from, but searching for, the God who made man in His own image.

The intent of this book is to follow the scarlet thread which runs through the history of this people from the time before the Mayan culture through the present day. The scarlet thread is blood:

Blood shed by the sword and blood shed upon a cross,
Blood shed through violence, resulting in death,
Blood shed in sacrifice in search of God, and
Blood shed by God, resulting in life.

Early in God's revelation of Himself, He made it clear to mankind that blood symbolized life, and that the shedding of blood represented death.[1]

Cain and Abel knew that God looked with favor upon Abel's sacrificial offering of a lamb, but had no regard for Cain's sacrificial offering of the fruit of the ground.

The principle of seeking God's forgiveness and favor through the shedding of blood was ingrained in mankind's spirit for the purpose of pointing us to Christ, who would be the perfect, spotless Lamb of God, giving His blood to cleanse our sin and provide a way for us to have a restored relationship with our Holy God.

While God's chosen people were being taught His plan of salvation through the Levitical sacrificial system, Satan was giving the pagan nations a counterfeit interpretation of their innate knowledge of the importance of a blood sacrifice. The God who created the heavens and the earth was replaced by many gods, as Satan's distortion of truth brought mankind into bondage to fear. His counterfeit gospel did not give life. Instead, it flooded the earth with a belief system that led to physical and spiritual death. God's chosen people even fell for the lie, making idols with their own hands and offering their children to the false gods.[2]

On the opposite side of the world from Israel, Satan developed his counterfeit into a culture and religion that the world still looks at with awe, blinded to its distorted image of the glory of man and God.

Christians have often been duped by Satan into playing God and calling whatever land they wanted to conquer their "Promised Land," misappropriating God's promises. It happened in South Africa. It happened in Mexico. Believing a lie, they all too often used the cross as a sword to conquer and keep the people of a desired land in submission.

But God is the Lord of all boundaries, and will allow Satan to go only so far before He uses some means to reveal His sovereignty, setting history back on His intended course.[3]

In 1517, Jerusalem was conquered by the sword of the Ottoman Turks. That same year, in Germany, Martin Luther tacked his ninety-five theses to a Wittenburg door, proclaiming the sufficiency of the Cross. Two years later, Hernando Cortes brought the cross and the sword to Mexico, which in time developed a syncretistic form of Christianity that is without light or hope.

Four hundred years later, the cross is cutting through the Christopaganism in Chiapas, separating a remnant of believers for the glory of God. These evangelicals are putting all their faith, no matter the cost, in the blood of Jesus Christ alone.

THE SWORD OF

PAGANISM

THE CROSS OF

SUPERSTITION

Chapter 1

A jagged edge of sunlight cut through the sagging door frame and lit the broken pottery, now painted with the little girl's blood. The shadow of her father tipped and rolled away with him, as another drunken stupor took him off to somewhere else, the walls of wooden slats breathing a sigh of relief at his departure. Pasquala lay still on the cool dirt.

She had wanted to make her mother smile. All day she had secretly worked on the pot. She'd often watched her mother crafting pots, sitting cross-legged in the dirt yard they shared with half a dozen bedraggled chickens. The clay had behaved nicely in her tiny fingers, and even her two young sisters left the new pot untouched to harden in the dry mountain air. She had carefully carried it in today, so focused, trying not to trip on the rocky path between the close houses, that she didn't see her father in the doorway.

Her head collided with the filthy bottle he held at his side. The bottle fell, spilling his precious posh onto the ground, which quickly drank the fiery liquid. Posh was the intoxicating drink made locally from fermented grain that ruled her father's life. Posh flowed during the sacred ceremonies and the festivals acknowledging the numerous Catholic and animistic deities. Pasquala's father was a slave to posh, and he had mortgaged their sheep, their chickens and their house to keep himself filled with holy inebriation.

Furious that his daughter had robbed him of the contents of his bottle, he struck out at her. His fist hammered against her head. Again and again he swung, taking out the fury of his own captivity on this worthless child of his, then breathlessly stumbling out to find more posh.

Pasquala laid unmoving, her broken skin, once ruddy like the fresh clay of her new pot, was now opened wide, bathing the ground in blood. Outside, a rooster crowed, though the sun had long since risen.

"Mama, please come home," she tried to think, as daylight slid to black.

———— ✳ ————

". . . They have built high altars to Baal . . .to cause their sons and daughters to pass through the fire unto Moloch, which I commanded them not, neither came it into my mind, that they should do this abomination. . ."
Jeremiah 32:35

". . . When you did not know God, you served those which by nature are not gods."
Galatians 4:8

THE SWORD OF PAGANISM

Several millenniums before Pasquala was weeping and bleeding over her broken spirit and pottery, her ancestors were trekking their way across Asia, across the frozen Bering Straits and down the western coast of the Americas. They could not have known that on the side of the world from which they had come, the Lord God had chosen a people, to make a nation of them, with the intention of demonstrating to the rest of the world how a substitutionary sacrifice would make peace possible between a Holy God and sinful men and women. Like that of Pasquala's ancestors, it was to be a religion revolving around ritual and sacrifice.

Though both great nations had ingrained in their hearts a recognized need for forgiveness, hope and justice, their method for working it out was quite different. One taught a sacrificial system demonstrating God's holiness and mankind's sinfulness, offering a way to approach God to receive forgiveness and to enjoy communion with Him. Pasquala's ancestors fulfilled that intrinsic need for God by developing their own religion based on a distorted substitution of many gods for the one true God. It was a mistake that still haunts Mexico today, perpetuating the emptiness of Mexico's people.

The History

This is not intended to be a history book, however it is important to invest a few moments reviewing Mexico's tumultuous history. Astute words from an historian still apply: "Mexico's history must be written with soft chalk, easily erased and corrected."[1] This is especially true in this age of new campaigns to identify and revive what was once considered a great culture. Even the overkill of cultural nationalism and excessive romanticism cannot negate the simple fact that hidden in the ruins of modern Mexico are evidences of an advanced culture, whose hieroglyphics and calendar for counting days and seasons far excelled those being used at that time by the Egyptians on the other side of the world.

Pasquala's predecessors were non-aggressive hunters, farmers and fishermen. It was only after they learned to cultivate corn that these wandering nomads were able to settle down in one place, with time to develop tools and the arts of basket weaving and ceramics. Corn is still the mainstay of their diet, which explains why it is still worshiped as one of their many gods.

Though historians list at least seven stages of Mexico's culture, three major kingdoms would eventually integrate their cultural strengths. Through time these kingdoms would lose their former greatness through specific cultural weaknesses, evolving into the Mexico of today.

The Olmecs - 1200 to 200 B.C.

While God's chosen people vacillated between worshipping God or idols, the Olmecs were settling on the soil and becoming the soul of what we know today as Mexico. As the Olmecs built pyramids as altars for human sacrifice to their gods, Homer wrote his Iliad and Odyssey, Socrates built arguments with words, and Alexander built an empire with the sword. The strength of the Olmec culture dissipated about the same time that Caesar and his armies were breaking down the strongholds Alexander had built.

The Mayans - 100 B.C. to 900 A.D.

While Christ was giving Himself as the Ultimate Sacrifice and building His Church, the Chinese were building a Great Wall and the Roman empire was being placed into the dustbins of history, the Mayans were developing their calendar and their knowledge of astronomy and mathematics.

Mayan culture was centered in Tikal, which had a population of over 100,000 and was set in a clearing of the Peten jungle in Guatemala. Palenque, in Chiapas, though smaller, was considered the scientific center of Mayan culture.

What happened to these advanced cultures? The Olmecs and the Mayans self-destructed as the people rebelled against an aristocracy that treated them as slaves. The cultures were further damaged by the practice of "slash and burn" agriculture, which created an ecological disaster that was exacerbated by earthquakes, locust invasions and other natural disasters.

The Aztecs - 1300 to 1500 A.D.

Inextricably linked to the Mayans are the Aztecs, the warriors from the north. As the Mayan nation was reduced to a remnant of powerless Indians, the Aztecs had a great influence on this Mayan remnant, and on all of Mexico, influences that extend to these last days of the twentieth century.

The Aztecs, for reasons unknown, were led to believe in their earliest formation that Mexico was their "promised land," promised to them by some ethereal being. Driven by prophetic zeal, these warriors and latent engineers turned a swamp into what is today the largest city in the world: Mexico City.

While the Crusades were shaking Europe, and a movement called the Renaissance began to take hold in Italy, the Aztecs came to power in Mexico.

They were personified in their last leader, Emperor Montezuema II. His control over his empire was never in doubt. His coronation was literally flooded by the blood of human sacrifice, and at his demise, the blood was still flowing. This despotic and oppressive ruler was powerful for two reasons. He was a very competent military leader, and he was a priest in the temple of the war god, Huitxilopochtle, the supreme god of the many gods of the Aztecs.

Montezuema's strength was also his weakness, however. As a priest, he lived in constant fear of his many gods. A comet's fiery tail or any cosmic event, such as an eclipse, struck fear in the hearts of all the Aztec priests. Knowing the prophecy of the land, he was frightfully aware that he was only a forerunner of a great war god who was yet to come. The Aztec's history described five successive worlds or suns. Each of the following worlds was named after the cataclysmic event that destroyed it:

1. Jaguar Sun Age: The earth was inhabited by giants and was destroyed when the giants were consumed by hoards of jaguars.
2. Wind Sun Age: The earth was destroyed by hurricanes and all humans were transformed into monkeys.
3. Fire Sun Age: The world was consumed by fire.
4. Rain Sun Age: A flood engulfed the world and all people were turned into fish.
5. Earthquake Sun Age: The world is to be destroyed by earthquake. Phoenix-like, the people will rise up out of the ruins with new leaders, new gods and a new culture.

There was a prophecy yet to be fulfilled. It was known by all that the great war god, Quetzalcaly, would return from the dead and save the world. He was prophesied to be a god who was, in their words, "white in skin, bearded, with a silver chest."

When a former law student from Spain named Hernando Cortez landed on Mexico's shores in 1512 with a beard and armored chest, Montezuema, shaking and trembling, believed Quetzalcaly had returned to reclaim his rightful bounty.

Though far from being a god returning to take back his kingdom, Cortez was considered one of Spain's most daring and cunning adventurers. Montezuema had good reason to tremble.

Montezuma's nation had come a long way from being a rattlesnake infested wasteland. The emperor ruled and exacted tribute from tribes scattered throughout much of what we know today as Mexico. Its capital, Tenochtitlan, now Mexico City, was built on a piece of swamp land, which through engineering feats still incomprehensible to many, had been transformed into a vast array of islands and lakes, temples and vast housing projects, forests of pine, oak and sycamore and miles of cornfields and plantations. It has been described as 2500 acres of sheer beauty with its crisscrossed geometric network of canals and embankments. There were adobe houses and stone buildings, which contained the population of over 100,000. All of this splendor, however, was dwarfed by temple-crowned pyramids built for human sacrifice.

The Aztecs, though, no matter how great their reputation as warriors, and Montezuma II, no matter how great his reputation as a military strategist, were no match for the Spaniard's weapons of war. The Aztec's bows and arrows, lancets, darts and heavy clubs with obsidian blades could not stand up to Cortez's crossbows, swords, knives, steel armor and artillery. Strategy, zealousness and patriotism would all collapse under the barrage of the most advanced weapons of death and destruction of that time. What the atomic bomb was to the Japanese, the musket and cannon were to the Aztecs.

Relentlessly advancing, Cortez entered Montezuma's capital in November 1519, confirming to Montezuma that the "great god of war" had returned for his empire.

The Aztecs lived by the sword and they perished by the sword. It was a lesson that went unheeded and unlearned by their conquerors. Even to secular historians their defeat carries unmistakable prophetic, if not apocryphal overtones. Historians still shake their heads in amazement at how Cortez, with only 500 men, could defeat an empire estimated variously from nine to twenty million. A major factor in the victory was not so much a tribute to Spain's prowess, but to one overriding factor in the minds of the Aztecs. Aztec soldiers had, as one historian put it, "a compulsive need to drag their enemies away alive for human sacrifice, instead of killing them on the spot and moving on." This practice was motivated by the profound need to deliver to the priests living sacrifices, so the gods could be fed their blood. Cortez could have been killed on several occasions had the Aztecs not been so set on delivering him to the priest alive, so that his beating heart could be cut out and held up to the sun god.

Nigel Davis in his book, The Ancient Kingdoms Of Mexico, writes the following:

"And if Cortez was not finally looked up to as a deity, he was in effect the instrument of god's will sent to destroy the Fifth Sun. Obsessed by their dismal cosmology, the ghastly omens came as no surprise to Montezuma and his soothsayers.

No Biblical prophet of doom could have foretold more relentlessly the end of this New World Nineveh. Never have the decrees of fate been so unerringly fulfilled."

The Black Thread

Though there were discernible differences between the Olmecs, the Mayans, and the Aztecs, there was one thread of commonality: a pagan religion fed by an all-consuming superstition. It permeated every aspect of their society from dawn to dusk, and through the night hours. It was believed that many of the gods could only be satisfied by the blood of a sacrifice: human blood.

The ruins of the Olmec culture, sifted by archeologists, give strong evidence that human sacrifice was an every-day practice. As early as the third century, their artwork depicts knives used to cut beating hearts from their sacrificial victims. Some of the artwork displays the heads of jaguars and eagles, many of them carrying human hearts in their mouths or beaks, dripping with blood.

The Mayans built what were first thought to be vast cities, but have been determined to be ceremonial religious centers where human sacrifice was a daily activity.

By the time the Aztec Empire reached its apex, its principal religion was the cult of a young god warrior named Juitzillopoctil, the sun god. The good news was that he was reborn every morning. The bad news was that he died every night and would not rise in the morning unless he was fed. His diet was limited to blood - human blood. War prisoners and peasants were his daily "bread."

The perpetrators of the flow of blood were the priests. Like the Pharisees and Sadducees of another land, they literally not only defined society but controlled it as well. There was no sharing of power with civil authorities. They had the power, and they never tired of exercising it. They were the mouthpieces for the many gods, many of whom they invented to extend their power. They were arbitrators of all things legal and illegal. The priests were the gate-keepers of any education the people might receive. They were the intelligencia, the scientists, and the authority figures that the common man groveled before, from birth to death, and all the long, difficult days of injustice in between. Their power was inescapable and unchallenged.

The priests luxuriated in the glories and comforts built by the scarred hands of their subjects, who in many cases would soon be the next to sacrifice their lives to the altars of the priest's egos, sensuality, and uncontrolled power. While their subjects lived in hutches with dirt floors, the priests lived in temples with paved courts.

Those first priests, in order to ensure homage to the gods and to perpetuate their power base, supervised the construction of gigantic mounds of dirt, on top of which offerings were made to the gods. They were offerings made up to a small degree by a portion of the laborer's crops, but primarily of the laboring peasants themselves.

What followed were theocratic governments. The common people had no power. When there was a drought, more sacrifices were made to appease the angry gods. When the drought ended, the priests told the people that the human sacrifices brought the rain, and now more were needed to keep the drought from returning.

The tragic irony was that the priests convinced the people that the highest expression of piety that one could make was to give their life as a sacrifice to the gods. Victims were sent as messengers to the gods, to demonstrate the reverence of the people. It was often considered an honor to make the sacred trip. With the same pious convictions, priests occasionally indulged in ritual cannibalism as a kind of pagan communion service, through which one might acquire the attributes of their enemy.

Life under the control of the priesthood might best be demonstrated in the rituals which took place regularly at the top of those pyramids that tourists admire so much today. A victim was chosen for any variety of reasons. It could have been an enemy captured in battle, a criminal or a peasant of no position. The victim, or victims, were taken to the top of the pyramid and made to lie face up, spread-eagle over a rounded stone, with their backs arched and their limbs held by four of the priest's assistants. The priest then took his sacred stone knife, and plunged it under the victim's rib cage. It was important that he remove the victims heart and hold it up with both hands while the heart was still beating, as an offering to the god of the sun.

Other gods demanded different rituals. The fertility god required the sacrificial victim, again one of the citizens chosen by the priest, to be shot full of arrows. The falling drops of blood symbolized the falling rain that would be needed to fertilize the wombs of the women and the fields of maize. Those who were "chosen" to honor the fire god with their sacrifice were drugged with hashish, and burned alive.

The depths of mankind's sinful nature is seen when we realize that, though separated by oceans, even God's chosen people were practicing a similar abomination. F. LaGard Smith in his book, Meeting God In Holy Places, describes what was happening in ancient Israel:

> "The Valley of Hinnon, as Gehenna was then known, was notorious as the site for sacrifices to the pagan god, Molech. Not just the ordinary sacrifices, mind you, but even child sacrifices. In this horrendous pagan practice, the worshiper would kiss his child and then place the child in the red-hot arms of the idol, inside of which was a continually burning fire. . ."[2]

Both cultures were attempting to appease their god through blood sacrifice. Blood sacrifice was designed by God for the Jewish nation as a way of covering their sins, thereby allowing them to commune with a holy God. The Aztecs attempted to appease their gods with the blood of human sacrifices. Instead of a pure system of sacrifice that demonstrated God's holiness and forgiveness, it was a system that demonstrated only the blood-thirsty and harsh nature of their priests and their many deities.

Some historians have suggested that one of the reasons for the demise of the Aztec cultures besides the natural disasters and the destruction of the environment, was a priesthood out of control, deleting their population through continuous sacrifices. As many as thirty to fifty thousand people might be sacrificed at one festival alone.

Of one thing we can be sure: the sword of paganism, yielded by the priesthood, cut through the very soul of a once thriving nation and sacrificed it to its many deities. The cross of superstition became more than the poor and oppressed could bear.

Instead of being washed by the blood of their sacrifices, their blood sacrifices literally choked the Aztec Nation to death.

———— ✳ ————

Pasquala's mother, Michaela, shuffled along the climbing highway, a basket full of blankets sitting heavily on her head. A rusted pickup truck lumbered by, kicking up a cloud of dust that settled on her woolen wares. Often she could get a ride along this 15-mile stretch from the city of San Cristobal to her little mountain town of Chamula, but today the dented truck already sagged beneath its load of weary human cargo.

Michaela made this trip at least three times a week. It was the only way she could provide her daughters with tortillas and a little fruit, with her drunken husband selling much of their food and mortgaging all they had for "that cursed posh." She crossed herself quickly and prayed the gods' forgiveness; it wasn't the posh itself that was cursed, she hadn't meant that, only that her husband was cursed for drinking so much of it.

The coarse black wool of her skirt chafed against her legs and ankles. It had been a bad day at the market square. Although the gods had blessed her with four healthy sheep who gave good thick wool, there was little benefit if no one bought it. She hated going to town. The arrogant Mestizos[3] piously scorned her presence, her native dress, and her discomforting reminder of their own heritage. They must be glad to have someone worse off than themselves, she thought, as Chamula greeted her from the next hilltop.

Of course, the tourists were worse. They would dismount their luxury tour bus, cameras and pale arms held tight against their bodies as if to guard against the plague. No need for them to worry - poverty is only transmitted through years of malnourishment. These white aliens looked away from the vendors, dismissing them with a wave of the hand, opting for the air-conditioned hotel lobbies. Blankets cost more there, but they looked the same, and they were sure to be cleaned first.

The sun was wavering on the mountain edge as Michaela trudged the last few steps through the fence of sticks, chicken wire and the cross that protected her house from stray dogs and evil spirits alike.

She stepped into the darkness of the doorway and froze in fear. Her daughter lay twisted on the floor among a puzzle of broken clay and drying blood, death-like in her stillness. Crashing down beside her, Michaela felt the small body tremble, still expanding and contracting with life. Her once important blankets now scattered on the dirt, she collected her daughter in her arms and stumbled out into the shades of twilight. Great coughing sobs competed with each breath as she carried Pasquala to the only hope she knew.

Shadows of night slithered around her as Michaela hurried along the rocky mountain path. Sharp stones bit at her cracked bare feet, but she felt nothing. She knew that she shouldn't be out here in the trees when darkness fell, for this was when the phantoms came. Winging out of caves and crevices, they left their homes in the underworld to rule the night. The phantoms came to her in dreams sometimes. Sent by a neighbor's curse or perhaps by her own disobedience, the phantoms watched her sleep with their evil eyes and wicked smiles, waiting for their chance to steal her soul forever. Now they held her daughter in their coils.

Who had Pasquala angered to earn this attack, Michaela wondered? Perhaps she angered someone at the well today, who cursed her in return. Perhaps Michaela had not burned candles long enough at the church yesterday. Perhaps it was only the will of Yajval Balamil,[4] the powerful Earth Lord.

Reaching the house of Marta, she lay Pasquala at the door, crossing herself fervently as she called out, "Marta!"

Marta was her sister. Marta was also a powerful healer.

She would know how to intercede for the soul of Pasquala. She would know how to appease Yajval Balamil and the evil spirits who fought to take her life.

Marta peered from within the mouth of her hut. "What is it, my sister?"

The panicky story poured from Michaela's mouth, laced with anguish and desperation. Hurriedly, Marta gathered up her charms and candles, her tools of intercession. Her blackened eyes fled wildly about, searching, then lit upon a chicken pecking cockroaches in the corner of her hut. Her toothless gums breathed the dreaded whisper and Michaela felt fear's jaws begin to tighten around her throat.

Picking up the trembling Pasquala, the sisters ventured once again into the deepening evening. In the arms of one was the sickly child whose soul was in the demon's hands, while in the other's arms the chicken screeched. . . a soul the demons soon would have.

As the last of daylight died, they reached the church in the town square. Bright blue paint framed ornate arches and the towering pinnacle, which boasted bells as loud as any in all of Rome's cathedrals. Towering over the poverty of San Juan Chamula, this scar of colonialism marked the hub of spiritual belief, imposing superstition and tradition on the minds of those who lived beneath its shadow.

As Marta led them through the heavy doors, the weight of darkness swallowed up their trembling heartbeats. A thousand candle flames carpeted the church floor, alive and dancing in the breath of the spirits. Michaela chanted softly beneath her breath, as she did each time she came to pray. Murmurs of only three other petitioners broke the silence, as most villagers came only in the daylight. Mother, broken daughter, and their advocate shuffled between the ceramic saints that stood as sentinels around the candle-lit church. Approaching a corner of the building, they stopped and crossed themselves three times, then knelt at a small altar.

The chicken in Marta's hand struggled violently, as if seeing for itself the eyes of the underworld. The healer reached into her bag, and drew out the candles. Michaela tried not to think of the cost. She knew the candles came at no small price. Yet what cost was too great for spiritual protection? She swallowed her doubts and crossed herself again. Placing one large candle in the center, and touching it with fire, Marta began to build a wall of flames around them. With each candle she set upon the floor, she prayed again for protection from the eye of the evil one, and huddled low behind its sacred barrier.

The glass-encased ceramic saints looked piously down upon them, unmoved by tears and flames. White as Europe's imagined purity, the icons remained aloof recipients of the faithfulness these dark-skinned natives offered.

Now protected by the candle's flame, Pasquala shuddered where she lay, as Marta drank deeply from a bottle of posh, then blew a mouthful through the flames. Dipping her finger into the holy liquid, she spread some on the child's lips, anointing her. Now Marta and Michaela chanted together, faces rising and falling to the ground with their voices, inviting the attention of Yajval Balamil.

Thus prepared, Marta drew a curved blade from her bag. Michaela clenched her eyelids in fear.

"Accept the soul of this chicken in place of the soul of my daughter," she pled in agony.

"Be at peace, oh earth god, be appeased by the gift of this chicken's life," chanted Marta.

The sea of candlelight froze as the spirits stopped to watch. The voice of the healer and an anguished mother wove together in a furious pitch of fervent supplication, then a flash of light, a plunge of steel, and the shriek of a chicken dying. Blood spilled from the chicken's body, pulsing over the altar stones and pooling around the melted wax. Dark and red beneath the fire, it seeped across the floor and touched the fingers of the child, who pulled away from it as if burned by the fire of hell itself. The sacrifice complete, the room offered no peace yet. With ceramic saints still frozen and Marta's chant now exhausted, the weight within the church threatened to suffocate its own attendants.

Michaela clutched her daughter's body and cried out for mercy. The candles were now melted to the floor, and vanished in a hiss as they fell into the pool of blood.

"Tsss." "Tsss."

Marta pronounced the child healed, and the sisters slowly made their way home.

Pasquala lay unmoving in her mother's arms, still unconscious.

It was many days before Pasquala was able to stand up and mind the house again. A fever's heat burned her forehead in a blood-red flush after the night at the church, and her condition worsened. Her mother carried her shrinking body to the creek each morning, bathing her in the dirty water, while the other women did their wash and shook their heads in pity. Many crossed themselves and burned extra candles, sufficiently warned by Pasquala's condition what may happen to their own children if they were not faithful to appease the gods.

But on the seventh day Pasquala awoke feeling better, and her forehead felt much cooler beneath Michaela's callused hand. Knowing her daughter was safe, she cried for joy, and sent a gift of stew and tortillas to her sister the healer. Surely it was worth the price of a chicken, she thought, forgetting all doubts of the nights before when her child tossed in the cold night air, seemingly unhelped by the sacrifice. In the secret part of her heart, Michaela wondered if the sacrifice only brought a worsened condition to her daughter, but with Pasquala's recovery, her doubts fell back into her subconscious.

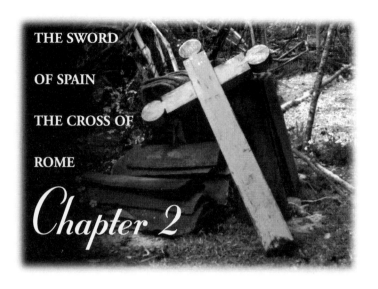

THE SWORD

OF SPAIN

THE CROSS OF

ROME

Chapter 2

> *. . . Should not the shepherds feed the flock?*
> *. . . Those who are sickly you have not strengthened, the diseased*
> *you have not healed, the broken you have not bound up, the scat-*
> *tered you have not brought back nor have you sought for the lost,*
> *but with force and with severity you*
> *have dominated them. . .*
>
> *Ezekiel 34:2-6*

> *Woe to you . . . hypocrites, because you travel on sea and land to*
> *make one proselyte, and when he becomes one you make him twice*
> *as much a son of hell as yourselves.*
>
> *Matthew 23:15*

THE SWORD OF SPAIN

While Indian blood was still dripping off the sacrificial altars, Cortez assured Spain that there would be an end to human sacrifice. He was incorrect. The new offering of Indian's bodies would be to Spain. Their blood would be shed to loose their souls from pagan ways, and to buy allegiance to the Church of Rome. Wielding the sword of Spain's armies and invested with the Vatican's authority, Latin America's new high priests brought the natives to their knees again, and laid on their back a cross nearly too heavy to bear. This was done in spite of the fact that the conquering Spanish, led by Cortez, were considered to be devout in their religious experience. Though often seen confessing their sins and praying, their piety was betrayed by the cruelty of their everyday actions against their captives.

Cortez and his priests' zeal was fueled by the fact that Spain had been granted extraordinary privilege by the Papacy in Rome, as a reward for chasing the Moslems out of Spain and for planting the "cross of Rome" in the New World. The King of Spain was considered to be a head of the Roman Catholic Church. Along with the accompanying power and prestige this conferred on Cortez's expedition, it also imposed the responsibility to establish the church as the pre-eminent authority in the Mexican colonization. It is little wonder that before long the most pervasive influence in what was now called New Spain was not Cortez, but the priests and the friars. Final authority now rested with both the sword of Spain and the cross of Rome. Because of their truncated and misappropriated powers, the destinies of Mexico and the Roman Catholic Church were forever linked.

Hispanic Christianity, it was believed, was unique in that Spain had been elected by God to be the instrument for the salvation of the world. It would be the first, but not the last time, that the Papacy gave a colonizing nation the two-fold authority to proceed with the twin virtues of colonizing and evangelizing for Rome. This process was officially called in Rome's language, "temporal and eternal, political and ecclesiastical, economic and evangelistic authority" over the newly captive land.

Cortez, demonstrating his allegiance to Rome, and undoubtedly urged on by his Roman Catholic priests, demanded that the Indians cast down their idols, stop all human sacrifice and abandon their many gods. On one occasion he put his mission in jeopardy as he destroyed some of the Aztec idols and replaced them with a statue of his own religion, given to him by his priests.

In reality, Cortez's occupation of Mexico was more of a military invasion and occupation than a mission. New believers were not converts as much as prisoners. The soldiers and priests introduced violent oppression and persecution, all in the name of Christianity.

The most damning criticism of the treatment of the Indians came from one of those priests, a Spaniard, born in Seville, who would eventually become the first Bishop of Chiapas, named Bartolome de Las Casas. He would not only become the first priest ordained in New Spain, but the first to speak out against the treatment of the Indians by both Spain and Rome. His first stinging indictment came in 1514, on Pentecost Sunday, when he severely condemned the treatment of the native people. Soon after, he freed his own slaves and began a vigorous campaign to redefine Spain's entire system of colonization, and more importantly, the system's relationship to Christian morality.

The most famous of his indictments was contained in a paper to his superiors entitled, "The Devastation of the Indies: A Brief Account."[1] His forward made him some powerful enemies as he wrote:

> "Were I to recount the vile acts committed here, the exterminations, the massacres, the cruelties, the violence and sinfulness against God and the King of Spain, I

would write a very big book, but this will have to wait for another time, God willing."

He then wrote of the attempts to bring the Indians into the Roman Catholic religion:

". . .nothing was done to incline the Indians to embrace the one true Faith; they were rounded up and in large numbers forced to do so. In as much as the conversion of the Indians to Christianity was stated to be the principle aim of the Spanish conquerors, they have dissimulated the fact that only with blood and fire have Indians been brought to embrace the Faith, and to swear obedience to the king of Castile, or by threats of being slain or taken into captivity. . . Spaniards have behaved. . . like ravening beasts, killing, terrorizing, afflicting, torturing and destroying the native people.

We can estimate very surely and truthfully that . . . with the infernal actions of the Christians, there have been unjustly slain more than twelve million men, women and children. In truth, I believe without trying to deceive myself, that the number of the slain is more like fifteen million. . ."

His book covers not only Mexico, but all of the lands of New Spain. The process was repeated in each colony, as de las Casas continues:

"The Spaniards did not content themselves with what the Indians gave them of their own free will, according to their ability, which was always too little to satisfy enormous appetites, for a Christian eats and consumes in one day an amount of food that would suffice to feed three houses inhabited by ten Indians for one month. And they committed other acts of force and violence and oppression which made the Indians realize that these men had not come from Heaven. And some of the Indians concealed their food while others concealed their wives and children and still others fled to the mountains to avoid the terrible transactions of the Christians.

And the Christians attacked them with buffets and beatings, until finally they laid hands on the nobles of the villages. Then they behaved with such temerity and shamelessness that the most powerful ruler of the islands had to see his own wife raped by a Christian officer. From that time onward the Indians began to seek ways to throw the Christians out of their lands. They took up arms, but their weapons were very weak and of little service in offense and still less in defense. (Because of this, the wars of the Indians against each other are little more than games played by children.) And the Christians, with their horses and swords and pikes began to carry out massacres and strange cruelties against them. They attacked the towns and spared neither the children nor the aged nor pregnant women nor women in childbed, not only stabbing them and dismembering them but cutting them to pieces as if dealing with sheep in the slaughter house. They laid bets as to who, with one stroke of the sword, could split a man in two or could cut off his head or spill out his entrails with a single stroke of the pike. They took infants from their mothers' breasts, snatching them by the legs and pitching them headfirst against the crags or snatched them by the arms and threw them into the rivers, roaring with laughter and saying as the babies fell into the water, "Boil there, you offspring of the devil!" Other infants they put to the sword along with their mothers and anyone else who happened to be nearby. They made some low wide gallows on which the hanged victim's feet almost touched the ground, stringing up their victims in lots of thirteen, in memory of Our Redeemer and His twelve Apostles, then set burning wood at their feet and thus burned them alive. To others they attached straw or wrapped their whole bodies in straw and set them afire. With still others, all those they wanted to capture alive, they cut off their hands and hung them round the victim's neck, saying "Go now, carry the message," meaning, take the news to the Indians who have fled to the mountains. They usually dealt with the chieftains and nobles in the following way: they made a grid of rods which they placed on forked sticks, then lashed the victims to the grid and lighted a smoldering fire underneath, so that little by little, as those captives screamed in despair and torment, their souls would leave them.

I once saw this, when there were four or five nobles lashed on grids and burning; I seem even to recall that there were two or three pairs of grids where others were burning, and because they uttered such loud screams that they disturbed the captain's sleep, he ordered them to be strangled. And the constable, who was worse than an executioner, did not want to obey that order (and I know the name of that constable and know his relative in Seville), but instead put a stick over the victims' tongues, so they could not make a sound, and he stirred up the fire, but not too much, so that they roasted slowly, as he liked. I saw all these things I have described, and countless others.

And because all the people who could do so fled to the mountains to escape these inhuman, ruthless, and ferocious acts, the Spanish captains, enemies of the human race, pursued them with the fierce dogs they kept which attacked the Indians, tearing them to pieces and devouring them. And because on few and far between occasions, the Indians justifiably killed some Christian, the Spaniards made a rule among themselves that for every Christian slain by the Indians, they would slay a hundred Indians."

Las Casas' final words to the King of Spain make even today's

Christians bow their heads in shame.

"Then Your Majesty will clearly see how those who govern her deserve to lose their governorship, in order to alleviate the conditions in these republics. And if this is not done, my view is that there is no cure for the infirmities of these lands.

Your Majesty will find out that there are no Christians in these lands; instead, there are demons. There are neither servants of God or of the King. Because, in truth, the great obstacle to my being able to bring the Indians from war-making to a peaceful way of life, and to bringing the knowledge of God to those Indians who are peaceful is the harsh and cruel treatment of these Indians by the Spanish Christians. For which scabrous and bitter reason no word can be more hateful to those Indians than the word Christian, which they render in their language as Yares, meaning Demons. And without a doubt they are right, because the actions of these Governors are neither Christian nor humane but are actions of the devil.

Hence, the Indians, seeing those vile actions of men so lacking in piety, they form the idea that the Christians obey the laws of the devil who is their God and King. And struggling as I do to persuade them of anything else is like trying to dry up the ocean. It gives them cause to laugh and to mock Jesus Christ and His law. And as the war-making Indians see the treatment meted out to the peace-loving Indians, they think it better to die in battle than to die many times under the dominion of the Spaniards. I know this, invincible Caesar, from experience. . .Your Majesty has more servants in the Indies than is known to Your Majesty, because there is not one soldier among the many here who does not publicly boast that when he bears in or robs or destroys or kills or burns the vassals of Your Majesty, it is because he wants to be given

gold for your Majesty. And this it would be well, O most
Christ Caesar, that Your Majesty let it be known, while
punishing some of them severely, that such services
which are a disservice to God, will not be accepted."

He sadly concludes:

"And today in all the Indies there is no more knowledge
of God, whether He be wood or sky or earth, . . . and
thus the nations have perished and are perishing without
the sacrament of the Faith."

Not every priest was a Bartolome de las Casas. There were
those who "extracted money and gift from the Indians by planting a fear of purgatory. On the visit to the priest the Indian never
came with empty hands." This and many other practices by the
priests who came to save the souls of the Indians condemned
many to something more than a perverted theology, but rather to
an eternal damnation.

To point this out as a historical fact is not an exercise in the
derogation of the Catholic Church, but stating what is a simple
matter of history, written primarily by Catholics. At the same
time, it would be patently unfair not to point out that, as is often
the case, there was a wide chasm between what the authorities of
Europe were ordering and how those orders were interpreted and
carried out on the front lines in Mexico.

THE CROSS OF ROME

De Las Casas was trying to persuade the soldiers in the New World and their leaders in the Old that "the way to win the Indians to the Faith was by showing a Christian spirit and returning to them what had been taken away. This is to be done 'without the noise of arms and soldiers, but with only the Word of God and the reason of the Holy Gospel.'" Then as now it was advice either largely unheeded, or bitterly opposed by his superiors.

Another friar, Padre Austin Cano, is quoted in a doctoral thesis done by Dr. Henry Aulie.[2] Padre Cano appealed to the Indians in the spirit of de as Casas when he wrote, "Our children and brothers, we came to this land because of our love for you. We didn't seek gold or silver or anything else. We only desired that you should know the one God and Lord in heaven and earth who is Jesus Christ by faith in whom you were to be saved. . . And those Spaniards who are charged with your care, whom you call your senores (lords), you should not call that, because only God is worthy of that title in heaven and earth, and the King also we address thus on account of his majesty, but no one else should be so addressed."

Thomas Gage, writing in the spirit of de las Casas and with a much greater understanding than many of his superiors said, "The Indians are very courteous and loving, and of a timorous nature, and willing to serve and obey, and to do good, if they be drawn by love, but where they are too much tyrannized, they are dogged, unwilling to please, or to work, and will choose rather strangling and death than life. They are very trusting and never were known to commit any robbery of importance, so that the Spaniards dare trust to abide with them in a wilderness all night, though they have bags of gold about them."[3]

Fray Ximenez writes that the Indians listened to the friars

with favor. On one occasion when the Indians responded readily, the friars baptized forty. This raised considerable discussion among the friars. Although some of them questioned the stability of the Chols, Ximenez adds that the friars continued their labors, and "God moved many to receive baptism."[4]

Padre Cano observed that there was both an openness to the message and bondage to their old way of life:

"... these barbarians do not resist the faith; they know that it is good and true, they know it from the preaching of the evangelical ministers who have labored much in these mountains, as also they are assured, the same Devil tells them that those who are not Christians know and believe; but their great idleness, laziness, lust and other vices has them so bound that it makes it difficult for them to observe the law of God. . ."

A similar mixed response of both favorable reception and withdrawal after making a profession is seen in the following entry by Cano:

"As the Lord was helping and confirming the preaching of the ministers, with these and other wonders, it gave much fruit, founding three villages with their churches and baptizing many souls, more than three thousand were counted, and among them were children who as soon as they were baptized rejoiced in God. . . among the older Indians there was much fruit although many left the faith, but many lived and died as Christians in those few years that the fathers were in the mountains. . ."

Unfortunately there was often a clash of words and policies, as Aulie writes, "It was a policy of the friars to round up Indians who had been baptized and resettle them (in towns) and in other places where they could conveniently catechize them." How did the Indians feel about this? They fled to the mountains and were pursued by the Spaniards. Weakened from the lack of food and cut off from water, they were overtaken and in a state of confusion, they capitulated."

Another side of the friar's methods and attitudes comes out in a report by Sanchez de Aguilar. He writes, ". . .a year ago in 1606, I discovered a cave with idols in the town of Chac, not far from the Church. . . entering in the Church I prayed for the errors and sins of the people who had been entrusted to me, where my sheep had abandoned the true Lord and the fountain of living waters to adore Astarto and Baal. . . I destroyed the altars in a moment and the idols with the help of an Indian Captain. I apprehended the delinquents and jailed them." This is quite different from the Pagans who burned their own idols and worshiped the one true God, after hearing Paul's message in love.

It was an attempt by the priests to make the Indians into Spaniards to satisfy Spain, and into Christians to satisfy Rome. They failed in both endeavors. The natives ended being bad Christians and "grotesque mimickers of Europeans," a bad foundation on which to build a modern Mexico.

The failure to understand the Indian's world view and consequently, the inability to communicate the true Gospel of Jesus Christ, resulted in what continues to be the root of today's problems in Chiapas.

Credit, though, must be given to those friars who faced the hardships of muddy trails, flooded rivers, heavy loads of food and drinking water, the heat by day, the cold by night, unfriendly villages, lack of shelter, exposure to torrential rains, insects, poisonous snakes and a host of other hardships. Aulie continues, "the dedication of these men to make the gospel known to the Indians cannot be questioned."

As time passed, the power of the church increased. Historians report that the Church controlled the education system, destroying what had been before and introducing its own culture. As their political power increased, the clergy became richer and less conscientious. Tithes, supplies for and receipts from baptisms, marriages, funerals and festivals, including the sacred alcoholic drink called posh, gave the church a massive revenue, and brought the people a new form of slavery.

Spaniards married Indian girls, giving birth to the Mestizos, the new favored landowner class, who also bowed to the church.

After several hundred years of subjection by a sword that was as deadly as the sapphire knife of the earlier priests, and a cross that was too much for anyone to bear, the people began to rebel. In 1910, the seeds of a popular revolution sprouted. From it came a new constitution in 1917, which was decidedly anti-clerical.

The church was viewed by the framers of the new constitution as blocking the path of progress. According to them, there could be no social revolution until the role of the church was changed. The constitution which was finally drafted and passed severely limited the control of the church. Marriages were declared a civil ceremony. Religious organizations no longer enjoyed special privileges. Priests were to be considered ordinary citizens, with no public worship outside the church walls. Clerics had to register with the government, and only a certain number could be from foreign countries.

The architect of the new constitution, thirty-three-year-old Francisco Magia, echoed the words of de Las Casas spoken four hundred years earlier, when he wrote, "I am an enemy of the clergy because I consider it the most baneful and perverse enemy of our country. What ideas can the clergy bring to the soul of the Mexican masses, or to the middle class, or to the wealthy? Only the most absurd ideas. . . tremendous hate for democratic institutions, the deepest hate for the principles of equity, equality and fraternity. . . are we going to turn over to the clergy the formation of our future? Fellow deputies, what morality can the clergy transmit as learning to our children? We have ample testimony; only the most corrupting and terrible morality."

His words may have been a bit all-inclusive, but they did seem to include at least the leadership of the religious community. The priests lost their white collars with the introduction of the new constitution, but they did not lose their power.

It was, and is, the priest that directs the lives of the Indians from baptism to burial. It was not difficult to entrap a naturally religious people with solemn ceremonies, tolling of chimes, tinkling of bells, burning of candles and incense, and multitudinous festivals, always dedicated to one of the saints.

Today, one sees that each village and city is built around a central church. Its cross spire, towering from the highest point on the landscape, is a graphic reminder to the people of the all seeing and far reaching power of the church.

———— ✳ ————

Pasquala leaned closer to the window of the bus. The hot vinyl seat burned her sweating legs, even through her coarse wool skirt. She closed her eyes to envision the village she was returning to. Had it been only four years? She counted back the miserable months in her mind. She was eight the last time her father beat her. Four years had not diminished the memory of his posh-breath, falling heavily from under the rim of his dirty straw hat.

Father left her on the floor that evening, and never came home again. A neighbor brought the news a week later. The old man had gone back to work in the fields the next day. Some rich man's field, Pasquala thought with deep bitterness. An illiterate twelve-year-old Tzotzil girl knew more about the politics of materialism and greed, without ever sitting in a classroom, than most educated girls would ever know. Her father often hired out to work for someone else, but only to make money to buy more posh, never to put more tortillas on their plates. Her father, reported their neighbor, had simply drunk himself to death.

The bus screamed up the winding mountain highway, straining under the load of too many passengers in its cramped quarters. Like many women, death to the man in the house was no real sadness, but perhaps even a secret celebration, at least until the cacique came to collect his debt. The house, the few sheep, even those wretched chickens had all been mortgaged by her father for the liquid that shackled him to his own grave.

Pasquala's sun-scarred face remained stoic, but even as she closed her eyelids, she could still see him. Curse him. Take his soul forever and enslave it, and may the blood of a thousand chickens never redeem it. With all the glory a village chief could muster, the cacique came. There was one at the head of every village. He was the local boss. Bought by corrupt government politician's money, his greatest betrayal was in bringing unanimous votes at every election. As long as the cacique kept the political machine well-lubricated, he was assured wealth and ultimate control. The house, the land, their livestock; the cacique wanted it all. And so, without speaking a word, mama gathered the remnants of their material lives and a few tortillas in a blue cloth, wrapped it around her back, took her three young daughters by the hands, and turned her back on Chamula.

Her eardrums strained with the bus engine, climbing with the altitude away from the coast. Just four years ago she was descending this road. That time, nausea won the battle, and she had vomited over the side of the pickup on which they rode. Now she was stronger. Four years of toil in the fields had given her one thing the landlord could not take away - a will to survive.

The coast. The hot land. The death land. Mama took them down the mountain to the hot lands, down to hell. Plantations there offered plenty of work to those who were willing to sell their freedom for slavery. But to lose your land is to lose your dignity. To work in another man's field is prostitution. Pasquala remembered the miles of sugar cane stretching out before them. She was sure that all the Indians on the continent couldn't eat as much sugar as those fields held. Why didn't they plant corn instead? One could live without sugar, yet there were many who died without corn.

The owner of the sugar cane plantation was a Mestizo. Most would call him a Mexican. In truth, his skin was dark, but his blood was white. Safe behind high walls topped with glass shards and nails, he lived in a mansion designed after some Spanish painting. Hanging baskets dripping with red flowers gave a handsome mask to the plantation house, hiding the generations of Indian blood that fertilized the rich coastal soil.

The day that her mother led them from the bus to the plantation gate hung vivid in Pasquala's memory. Chamulans were a proud people, but to enslave themselves to a Mestizo was their only means of survival. This survival could be a disease, and Pasquala had watched it kill her mother. The owner, or Jefe as they called him, emerged from the house to look them over. Sliding his hat back on his thick black hair, his eyes roamed over Michaela, assessing, pricing, evaluating. How much cane could she carry without that baby at her breast? Three girls, no boys. A shame. But they were small, and wouldn't eat much. Young and beautiful, the older girl might even be fit to give him pleasure some day.

He looked carefully in the eyes of new workers. There was anger there, yes, even desperation. "Good," he thought, "Anger makes a hard worker." Only when there was despair were they worthless, when there was resignation to the inevitable. There is a small but significant difference between desperation and despair. Desperation comes from the clinging hope that living is the better way. Despair comes from the realization that death is certain, imminent and perhaps, even a relief. He had seen his workers succumb to despair many times. It was a shame really, but in the history of the world all profit has a cost, and the Indian made a convenient currency.

No words were spoken between this lord and his new servants, for though they shared a not-so-distant heritage, they did not share a language. For Pasquala, he did not need an interpreter for his heart spoke without his mouth. She did not need to lift her eyes to his face to know what he was saying. Rather, the writing was on his shining boots. Carefully polished by the hands of some Indian boy, who, kneeling in subservience, was not considered worthy to wash even the feet of his master. Instead, the boy would shine the boots which trod upon the dignity of every indigenous man. Pasquala remembered seeing her own reflection in the polish of the Jefe's boots.

Lurching onward, the bus carried her body away and her memory back.

They lived together with the other workers in a shelter, out of sight of the hacienda. Banana leaves lashed together with fiber cord, and flung over flimsy wooden poles made a crude dormitory roof. The shelter had no walls; the best place to string your hammock was in the middle, where at least the driving rains of the wet season couldn't pour in and flood your few hours of rest. As there were no barriers between the open night and those sleeping in the shelter, crude crosses of cane stalks were constructed and hung around the roof to ward off the phantoms who watched thirstily from the darkness.

Each morning, before the sun bled through the black sky, they awoke. An early start was critical. More time in the fields meant more loads of cane, and more loads of cane carried into the barns meant more pesos. Early mornings and grueling work was not anything new to these people, whose very souls were rooted in the soil of their land.

The best time to work was before the sun climbed too far into the sky. Although darkness was an enemy to be feared above all others, the sun often proved to be an adversary as well. Relentless, it dangled in the sky over the cane fields, a torch that made the skin shrivel and crack in protest.

When they first arrived, Pasquala's task was to carry her infant sister in a cloth-wrap on her back, and to be sure that her fragile skin was shielded from the sun's wicked glare. Snakes were another enemy lurking in the shadows of the cane field. Although the large rats that ran between the feet of the workers usually satisfied the snakes, an infant who slept unguarded on the cane field floor stood a very real danger of being bitten. While her mother still tried to burn candles regularly, and chanted every morning, the isolation of the fields prevented them from being as faithful in appeasing the spirits. This made it even more important to be watchful for evil, whether from the heat, snakes, or other dangers in the field.

Despite threats of disease and natural enemies, Pasquala feared the planes most of all. She still remembered the first time an airplane flew over the cane fields, frosting the crops and workers with fertilizer. Pasquala had never dreamed of such a creature, even in her most horrible nightmares. Roaring in a deafening voice, the metal monster swooped down upon them, swirling the sea of sugar cane in its wake. Surely this was the end - some creature sent by Yajval Balamil from the underworld to destroy the unfaithful Indians who had forgotten him in their devotion to the field work. They would all meet a terrible end here, Pasquala thought, as she lay over her baby sister, shielding her from the danger above. The flying dragon breathed a cloud of death that whispered downward through the sunlight, settling on the cane stalks and the worker's skin.

She couldn't have known then that it was fertilizing chemical that fell from the sky, setting her skin on fire, itching and burning wherever it touched and leaving red marks for several days. The fertilizer plane would return many times after that first encounter, but Pasquala never felt any less afraid. At times, after a particularly thick mist of fertilizer fell, someone would become sick with a disease of the breathing. More than one time, a worker who became sick died soon afterward, their lung tissues burnt and corroded by the chemicals.

Weeks in the fields became months, and though the rainy season came and went a second time, still they did not stop working to observe the festivals honoring the spirits or the saints. Pasquala noticed her mother's back beginning to take the shape of an old woman's back, though her mother was not an old woman. The heavy bundles of cane often weighed seventy pounds, and bent her mother over to face the ground as she walked up and down the trail to the barn over and over again. Michaela only stopped to rest three times each day, long enough to lift her infant daughter to her sweaty chest, giving her life. How she was capable of giving life, when she felt that living had been taken from her, she never understood.

No sooner had her baby sister learned to take her first timid steps than Pasquala began to work in the fields next to her mother. With Juana, her six-year-old sister assuming the task of minding the baby, and Pasquala laboring in the field, they could earn almost a dollar a day. However, the Jefe kept this money for them, paying them only enough each week to buy a few tortillas and bananas in the market place. This seemed to be a fair arrangement, as the girls and their mother had no immediate need for the money.

But as years passed and the cane loads grew heavier, and the attacks of the fertilizer plane came more frequently, Michaela began to grow anxious about the money they were breaking their backs for. Behind the broken skin and burning eyes, she walked each step of every cane load dreaming of the day when she would have enough saved to buy a small piece of land to call her own, ending this humiliating enslavement.

Looking back from the seat of the bus, Pasquala thought of that day. The last day.

Early in the morning, as the darkness began to release them from its presence, her mama awoke. She climbed out of her hammock, wrapped her cleanest skirt around her hips, and tied her hair back with a string of yellow and orange beads. Kneeling on the ground, she faced the direction of the hacienda and placed five candles on the ground in the shape of a cross. As the candles wavered beneath the pulse of dawn, she chanted for protection from the eye of evil, and begged the mercy of Yajval Balamil.

"Mama, are you not going to the fields today?" Pasquala asked curiously, recognizing an air of urgency about her mother.

"No child, today we go to see the Jefe."

She said no more. Crossing herself, she stepped around the cross of candlelight that hovered over the ground, and led her girls down the path to the Jefe's house.

They walked for an hour in complete silence, until together they stood before the hacienda gates. Pasquala shivered as her mother rang the bell.

"What is it?" demanded a servant, scowling at them through the iron gate. Although he was one of their own, the servant had acquired the callused demeanor of a superior, so as not to jeopardize his position in the house by some note of sympathy to his brothers and sisters in the field.

"May I speak with Jefe?" Michaela began, undaunted by the betrayal of the doorman.

"Jefe has many concerns and does not wish to be troubled by field workers," retorted the servant confidently, yet not daring to look them in the eyes.

"It is about the matter of our wages, and I will stay here until your master is able to speak with me." Michaela allowed anger to singe the edges of her voice. How dare this boy disrespect an elder with his arrogance? Servant to the king or slave to his fields, it made no difference by the standards they both knew.

The servant's pride trembled slightly at the reference to "your master" and turned back to the house to relay the message.

Pasquala felt sweat running in the lines of her mother's hand, and she gripped it tightly. Angry mother and fearful child stood hand in hand to face the Jefe.

For two hours they stood unmoving at his gate, until finally he emerged from the safety of the house, wiping food off his lips with a white handkerchief.

"What do you want, Woman?" he snapped, flicking his cigarette through the gate. It landed at the feet of Michaela, who would not let her eyes drop to meet it.

"Sir, for many months, and even years, we have diligently served you in your fields. You have withheld our wages, promising to give them to us in the future. Now, Jefe, we would like to collect the money we have earned." She spoke directly, without allowing her voice to falter.

The Jefe stared through the iron bars of the gate, letting his eyes drift from her direct stare to the cigarette in the dirt at her feet, and back to her eyes. Reaching into his pocket, he pulled out two bills and examined them. He crumpled them up and tossed them through the gate, forcing her to stoop to pick them up.

Four hundred pesos. About sixty dollars. For two to three years of enslavement. Sixty dollars to purchase the strong back she broke for him. Sixty dollars to pay for the pride she sacrificed the day she first approached this gate. Sixty dollars. Four hundred pesos.

This time her voice stretched to control itself. "Jefe, we have worked now three long years. You have given us only enough money to buy a few tortillas and bananas each week at market. We have served you in your fields and not complained. Jefe, we want the payment you promised us."

"You ungrateful pagan," the Jefe's voice made no attempt to control itself. "You have lived on my land, under a roof I put over you. You have lived these three years without starvation or disease. Now you ask for money from me. Go back to the fields, and do not infuriate me with your whining!"

Pasquala felt her bones crack in the grip of her mother's hand, but she did not hear them over the drumbeat of her heart.

Michaela shrugged the years off her back and straightened to her full five feet. Every beating her husband dealt her, every nail that hunger pounded into her belly, every pound of sugar cane that ever broke her spine, the terror of the night and the horror of the day all reached up within her and put their claws around her throat. Like a chicken with the healer's fingers round its neck, she erupted with desperation.

"You are like the white man! May you be forever cut off from your ancestors in this land. May the ground close up her womb to you, and may you have to taste the blood of every native heart that bled upon your soil. May the Virgin Mother visit vengeance upon you by day and the spirit of Yajval Balamil steal you children by night. May the blood of all your chickens never pacify the underworld, and the fire of all your candles never illuminate the darkness. May phantoms scorn the high walls of your house, and let evil always strike you in your home."

Her hatred now loosed, she spit on the ground, and turned her back on his presence. The tears of her daughters watered the path back to the workers' shelter, and Michaela was silent.

The cross of candles still burned where they had left it, burning low in its dissolving vigil.

As Pasquala sat weeping on the bus, all she could think of was the smell of the candles.

They came for her mother that night. Night was smothering the shelter when the Jefe's men emerged from the trees. Maybe her mother knew they would come, maybe she didn't. In any case, she didn't try to run. She held her daughters until they dragged her clear of them.

"The Jefe is boss! The Jefe is boss! The Jefe is boss!" they screamed over and over through clenched teeth, as if afraid of themselves. The field workers stared, possessed by the scene, unable to look away.

The men put a gun to her mother's face. "The Jefe is boss," they screamed again, and pulled the trigger. There was an instant of silence before the blast of the gun. The cross of candles caught its breath, and Pasquala's screams were swallowed by the quiet. Her mother's eyes were closed. Death stood waiting.

Then blackness choked her. The cross of candles drowned itself flame by flame, until only a dying breath of smoke hovered over the last smoldering wick.

The bus came to a stop. The ride was over.

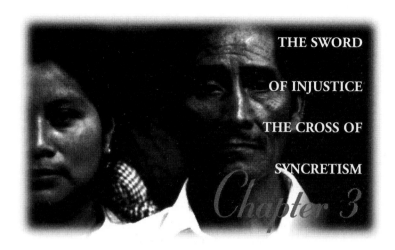

THE SWORD

OF INJUSTICE

THE CROSS OF

SYNCRETISM

Chapter 3

O Lord, how long shall I cry, And You will not hear?
Even cry out to You, "Violence!" And You will not save?
Why do You show me iniquity, And cause me to see trouble?
For plundering and violence are before me;
There is strife, and contention arises.
Therefore the law is powerless, and justice never goes forth.
For the wicked surround the righteous;
Therefore perverse judgment proceeds.

Habakkuk 1:2-4

THE SWORD OF INJUSTICE

The nature of human sacrifice, though continued long after Cortez, has been transformed into something more "humane." No longer are beating hearts cut out and their blood offered as food to the sun god. The stone altars and sacred knives in the hands of the pagan priesthood have been superseded by forced labor and forced religious beliefs, ministered by those who call themselves the "priesthood of the believers." The swords of both priesthoods cut deeply, recklessly and interminably into the psyche, pride and culture of the Indians.

The Indian's survival instincts first drove them to scatter in retreat into the rural mountain region that we know today as Chiapas - 73,877 square kilometers of rivers, valleys, rain forests, caves, lakes, waterfalls, salty marshes, and palm trees. The survivors have multiplied into a population of 3.2 million people.

The ethnic makeup of Chiapas is comprised of the Tzotsils and Tseltals in the center of the state, the Chujes, Choles, and Zoques in the north, the Tojolablas, Mames, Cakchiquels and Mochoes in the south, and the Lancandons in the eastern rain forest.

Though they are separated by many different types of terrain, all of the tribes survive on corn, beans, squash, potatoes, tomatoes, and a lot of faith. Their religious beliefs vary somewhat from one group to another, but most all incorporate their Mayan traditions and beliefs with heavy doses of Roman Catholicism, the predominate religion. The capital of Chiapas is Tuxtla-Guitierres, and the spiritual center is the city of San Cristobal de Las Casas, named in 1528 after the first Bishop of Chiapas, Bartolome de las Casas.

Chiapans are proud of their Mayan culture, but frightened about their future. Once again, they are experiencing the piercing and slashing of the sword of injustice, now being wielded by a nearly irredeemably corrupt Mestizo government, and a church awash in hopeless Christopaganism.

Although it is difficult to measure the mental suffering imposed upon Chiapas' Indians, the physical injustices are more easily calculated. Chiapas supplies fifty-five percent of Mexico's hydroelectric power, yet two-thirds of the indigenous Indians, after a hard day's labor, return home to a shack lit only with candles or a kerosene lantern.

Fifty-four percent of them suffer from malnutrition. The average family of four eats one sparse meal a day, cooked over a wood fire. Though the father will have worked from dawn to dusk so that Chiapas can be the major producer in Mexico of coffee, cattle and corn, his salary of twenty pesos a day will place such food on their tables only on very special occasions, and never in abundance. His weekly salary will be less than the tourist in San Cristobal will spend for coffee and croissants in the morning, before boarding an air-conditioned bus to visit the ruins of his ancestor's culture, oblivious to the human ruins passed along the way.

Mothers are considered fortunate if they live beyond their life expectancy of thirty-eight years. Every year 15,000 children die of preventable disease, of which they could be cured if they lived in San Francisco or Berlin, or even Mexico City. Nearly half of the population of 3.2 million Indians receive no medical care whatsoever, except for that given by a witch doctor.

Fifty-nine percent of Indian children receive no formal education. Kindergarten for girls is learning to sell hand-made souvenirs to the tourists in the city square, until they are ready to become a child bride and continue the cycle. Their brothers will soon set aside their textbooks, if they have any, to journey with their fathers to the fields or the rock quarries, or to the forest to cut trees, never to return to school. They will become victims of "forced illiteracy," eventually marrying a child bride and completing the vicious cycle of poverty.

Is it any wonder that Chiapans become bitter when someone in their village who can read a newspaper tells them that their president, who promised to make serious efforts to remedy these injustices, receives a salary of $8000 per month, compared to the villager's $35 a month, and that he also has a secret discretionary fund of $86 million dollars, with no accountability as to how he spends it? Though the villagers might be illiterate they are aware, from years of experienced injustice, that their other elected officials are guilty of similar discrepancies. Cortez had said, "Spain has a disease that only gold will cure." Mexico is still infected.

The people of Mexico City do appear to be proud of their Indians. There are giant murals on government buildings, and plaques that extol the bravery of the Aztecs. There are museums filled with artifacts of the great Mayan culture. Maybe, the Indians conclude, it is true that Mexicans are proud of their past, but ashamed of their present.

And well they should be, as in reality three million Indians live as a conquered race, victims of poverty and discrimination. Their hope for something better decreases every time a hectare of land is taken from them, and every time they are betrayed by policies inaugurated between election campaigns.

"Assimilation" was the policy that President Cardenas, himself part Indian, propounded in 1930 when he said, "Our indigenous problem is not to maintain the Indian as an Indian, nor of 'Indianizing' Mexico, but it lies in how to 'Mexicanize' the Indian, while respecting his blood, preserving his emotion, his love for the land and his unbreakable tenacity." The promises were not new but they were generally forgotten after he won the presidency, just as they had been in the past. "Mexicanization" became like so many eloquent shibboleths since then, a policy more akin to disappearance than assimilation.

Earlier in 1910, the government had "respected his blood" by drafting Indians into the army and giving them rifles to fight for the cause of freedom. However, after the revolution, the Indians had to turn in their weapons and received in their place, from the government and the Bishop who played a major role in enlisting them, a plaque and a flag of the lady of Guadalupe. There was never an effort to "preserve their emotion," or to give back their land. The only thing they still had was their "unbreakable tenacity," which was continually smothered by false promises or physical suppression.

Many of the Indians may be illiterate, but they do know their heritage. They know that during the Spanish conquest their ancestors fled to the jungles, mountains and deserts. They occupied what they called, "zones of refuge." They lived for a short time under the false assumption that they would be able to retain this land as their own. Their land became their mother, their sustainer, the home of many of their gods. It was a part of them they thought could not be taken away. They may have been chased away from their homeland, but always they would be looking back, waiting for their gods to chase the interlopers off so that they could return. Their great god had promised that this land was theirs. The land was more than a territorial base, it was a major part of their identity and religion. Indians could not live where "their land" was not dirt, brush, rocks, stones and trees. Land was sacred, and they were lost without it.

This precious piece of real estate, though by constitution legally theirs, held vast haciendas, cattle ranches, and coffee and cocoa plantations. Forty-five percent of the arable land was controlled by one percent of the people, the mestizos, the descendants of immigrants from Europe, and special friends of the PRI, the ruling political party. If the Indians had any land, it was some rocky parcel that cattle could not graze on, and where coffee and cocoa would not grow. There were times when the Indians, with arduous labor, using man-made hoes and sticks, would clear a piece of land to make it usable. Though legally it had been given to the indians, the mestizos would claim it as theirs and turn it into a cattle ranch, or cultivate it for coffee or cocoa. If they did not move further into the jungle and leave the land, the governor would send in troops to remove the Indians, while the issue of ownership was taken to court for a decision which was never made. In the meantime during litigation, the mestizos had what they called the White Guards, which were hired hoodlums who, under the direction of the landowners, would intimidate the Indians into leaving. It is the same today. Human rights organizations report that hundreds of Indians have been killed in the last few years, but their murderers, if arrested, usually receive only official reprimands.

The Indian's arable land has decreased while the mestizo's cattle raising areas have tripled, swallowing up what was once jungle and Indian land.

In case the Indians might be tempted to take to the streets in protest, a law was enacted by the Chiapas state Government, Criminal Code Article 225, stating that "any person who seizes land by obstructing common arterial, land, building or public squares can be sentenced to prison for four years."

Sadness and heaviness of heart pervades the culture, as does lack of compassion and shame by those imposing these terrible injustices. Though it is true that the signs in the city of Ocosingo have been removed that read, "INDIANS AND LIZARDS NOT ALLOWED," as though Indians passing through their gates would infect the entire city, other injustices continue.

If there is any truth in the saying, "The "wheels of justice grind slowly," then one must accept the fact that the wheels of injustice grind even more interminably. The Indians of Chiapas have earned the right to cry out, "How long, oh Lord, how long?"

"You shall have no other gods before Me.
You shall not make for yourself any carved image,
or any likeness of anything that is in heaven above,
or that is in the earth beneath,
or that is in the water under the earth;
you shall not bow down to them nor serve them.
For I, the Lord your God, am a jealous God,
visiting the iniquity of the fathers on the children to the third and
fourth generations of those who hate Me,
but showing mercy to thousands,
to those who love Me and keep My commandments."
Exodus 20:3-6

THE CROSS OF SYNCRETISM

The Indians of Chiapas carry many crosses on their callused shoulders. One of the heaviest is syncretism, defined as "a combination of different forms of religious belief or practice." More specifically, it is the "unconscious tendency of the conscious attempt to undermine the uniqueness of a specific religion by equating its elements with those of other belief systems."

Syncretism, as it pertains directly to Chiapas, is defined by veteran missionary Dr. Henry Aulie, as "the blending of ancient Mayan understanding of the spiritual world with certain practices of Roman Catholicism that were introduced by the Spaniards who entered Chiapas."

The following illustration of syncretism is given to demonstrate how it is at the core of the problems in Chiapas, affecting all aspects of life everyday life.

A single path out of the jungle winds its way down the side

of a hill. It weaves through brush, across a stream and along dusty, unmarked paths. Eventually, it widens, as the marks of bare feet in the mud and dust are joined by the hoof marks of a mule, and the tire marks of a bus or truck. A hut appears on the side of the road. Crushed rock now widens the road's approach to a typical village. The size of the village's focal point is dictated by the number of people who come into the streets of the village to sell or trade their wares. Usually on a high piece of ground, standing like a sentinel, is the local Roman Catholic Church, its ornate, white-washed facade standing out in stark contrast to the buildings that surround it. A large cross in its center silently gives its own message. Two bells hang silently on each side of the cross. Beside them are two large loudspeakers. The church's shadow quietly invades a large square with a small fountain in the middle.

Merchants remove boards from the fronts of small hutches that mark the boundaries of this twentieth-century temple. Almost imperceptibly, a market place begins to appear catering to the needs of residents and pilgrims alike.

Somewhere behind the scenes an unseen hand takes hold of a rope and begins pulling. The bell comes to life, reminding the people not only of who they are, but to whom they belong. Its first peal announces a new day. Everyone knows what they are to do. It will ring throughout the night and the day with the same results.

Slowly, there is life in the village square, as residents are joined by those who have trekked for hours or days. At the door of the cathedral a guard, dressed either in black pants and a white shirt, or a black goat's skin skirt and black shirt, with a sweat-stained straw hat on his head and a staff in one hand, reaches out with the other to collect the entrance fee.

Inside, a pervading darkness is violated only by burning candles. Overlooking the sanctuary are statues of saints. There are no pews. People sit on the floor, facing an ornate altar that extends from the floor to the ceiling. The group includes women holding children in each hand and on their backs, the infirm, a merchant, and a few young men. A group of peasants, tired from hours of travel, moves to the front of the church. There are only whispers and murmurings. There is no singing. They stand in line for a few moments, then give their "widow's mite" to buy one large candle and a handful of short skinny ones.

Slowly, with resigned determination, they find a vacant place to squat on the floor. With their legs folded under them, they bow several times toward the front of the church and to one of the plaster saints surrounding them. First, they take small candles and put them in a straight horizontal line in front of them. Perhaps someone in the village has given them the evil eye and they are now controlled by the devil, or someone is going to kill them, or their third child is sick and may die like the other two, or it is time for the corn to sprout and it has not yet come. There are as many reasons for lighting candles as there are worshippers in the cathedral. These little candles block evil, which they call the "black eye of the devil." They light the candles one at a time, tip them, put a drop of wax on the floor and place the candle in it to set up a line in front of them. They will then take the large candle, which represents the person or object of prayer, or is a gift to God, or it is itself believed to be one of the many gods that they will pray to. Some will take a mouthful of a locally brewed alcohol called posh. This is a highly fermented drink that is at the center of the religious fiestas. It is a sacred drink that is worshiped as a god in its own right. They will not swallow it, but instead will spit it on the candles, as an offering to the gods, and as a plea to remove the evil that has taken over their lives.

Another small group is clustered in a circle at the back of the altar. There are no candles here. A small ceramic bowl is removed from a basket. A knife is drawn from a sheath attached to a belt. Someone reaches into another basket, and there is a brief scuffle as a chicken is taken out and brought inside the circle. There are a few prayers and then a brief squawk. Then silence, as all stare at the center of the circle. The bowl, now filled with blood, is lifted above the heads of the participants, while the worshippers, eyes closed, face the altar and pray. After a short period of time, there is a bustle amongst them, and the chicken carcass is placed back in the basket, leaving behind only the empty vessel, stained with blood.

If a sick child later lives, the credit goes to the god. If the child dies, they realize that next time, they must buy more candles and come to pray more often. If the rains come and there is food for a time, it is because of their worship of the rain gods. If the drought continues, it is because they did not pray enough to the rain gods. If the god of rain remains angry, more trekking, more candles and more prayers will be necessary. Their burden is only relieved by a fiesta, where they will swallow their posh and drown their miseries for a few hours.

The worshippers continue to come all day. They light their candles and they pray to their gods. In the end, though, they all give ultimate obedience to their predominant idol, the most richly clothed of the many, Our Lady of Guadalupe, the Virgin Mary.

The bells ring, the murmuring continues, a heavy haze of smoke creates an oppressive, surrealistic atmosphere extending from the church's facade to the city square and down the many trails that lead from the village.

This scene is repeated in villages all across the land.

This is the church of Chiapas, the center of power, dictating to the people not only what they are to believe, but how they are to act out those beliefs, not just when to laugh, but when to cry. They will be its constant attendant from the time they enter the world, gasping for their first breath, to the time they leave this world exhaling for the last time, and every moment in between.

This is the Church.
This is Chiapas.
This is Mexico.
This is Syncretism!

Syncretism's successful blending of paganism and Christianity depends heavily on ritual for its survival and growth. Ritual, that symbolic expression of people's deepest feelings about their gods, is directed by individuals with different roles.

At the top of the hierarchy is the priest. It is his duty to keep alive the rituals of serving the images, of lighting candles, of coordinating fiestas and of offering prayers to the gods in times of need.

Aulie gives a vivid description of not only the role of the priests, but the forms of their rituals, in the words of an informant who writes, "When the sky is clear they worry because the corn no longer grows well. So they think about asking for rain. The elders, under the direction of the priest, will ask an image to send rain. They take candles to the images and begin to worship, saying, 'Have pity on us.' They vainly suppose that rain will come by lighting candles. First they line them up. When they are lined up they ask for rain, hoping that it will come. Sometimes it happens that the sky gets cloudy. When rain comes, they are very happy. They say to one another, 'See, we were able to do it! God heard our worship. Rain has come.' If rain does not come, they meet together again. They decide how to again ask for rain. Sometimes when rain still does not come they go to the middle of a stream where they set up a cross so that rain may come." If the rain comes, the image gets the credit, of it does not come the people get the blame. They have sinned, they do not pray enough, they must sacrifice more. It is an endless enslaving cycle of condemnation and guilt.

Occupying the second level of spiritual hierarchy, with power over the minds and hearts of the Indians, are the Spiritists. This according to Aulie is "an assumed role, not an office to which one is appointed." A man who desires to practice spiritism and believes he is adept for it dedicates himself to communicate with the spirits and propitiate them. Another name for a spiritist is "one who talks to the cross." He is believed to be able to cure an illness, cast a curse, discern the culprit in cases of blame, bring rain, procure a good crop, etc. Spiritists normally consult the spirits inside caves, since that that is where it is believed the spirits live.

Next in the line of the plethora of ritual providers is the shaman, or witch doctor. He is the specialist in the community who is looked to for knowledge of the laws which control nature and magic, and for skill in the practical arts of healing, cursing, and bringing favorable weather for the crops. The acts which he performs are only means to the desired end that is expected to follow. The practice of shamanism is therefore quite different from the acts of religion which are "themselves the fulfillment of their purpose." The shaman may be a man or a woman and is believed to be specially qualified for the office if he has two rings of hair on the top of his head. A missionary's wife tells of an Indian helper who once saw a person with two "cowlicks," (rings of hair) and he wanted to kill him because this was a sure sign that he was indwelt by an evil spirit.

The shamans are believed to have the power to invoke spirits. They are called to perform the ritual of divination when it is suspected that an enemy has caused a sickness. There is a specific ritual in which a candle is lit and placed in the house of gods in order to ask who is responsible for the sickness. The sick person is told to send for a quart of liquor. The shaman puts a kernel of white corn in the bottle of liquor, then turns the bottle upside down. The image of the man who caused the trouble is supposed to appear on the corn. If he has acted from malice, the image will hang his head. Only a shaman can perceive who it is. He will order the killing of a pig, turkey or chicken. Then the person is supposed to get well. Sometimes it happens that the one who caused the sickness will be killed. Much depends on how the shaman handles the case who is the accused. Hostilities arise when the shaman makes false accusations.

As Aulie points out, "Shamans are distrusted and feared. Some have been murdered. One told how that when one of his wives died, it was only with great difficulty that he was able to find men to dig a grave. One of the two men who helped dig the grave was a relative and an evangelical. The shaman is feared and hated because of the power for evil he exerts on people or crops by invoking evil spirits."

Though some groups in Chiapas are less involved in syncretism than others, nearly all believe in supernatural forces which define each day, what they do, what they think, how they act, their present and their future. It is a powerful force, which creates fear and hopelessness, and makes them amenable to the addition of more deities to control their lives.

There are both friendly spirits and evil spirits. The principal deity in the pantheon of friendly deities is the sun, literally "our holy father." He is believed to be all powerful, and lives forever. This is the deity that needed, in earlier days, human blood to give him strength to come up the next day. He has a body and yet pervades all the world. He judges rightly. How close a pagan belief can come to truth is seen in the belief that this great god decided that Jesus Christ should be born of Mary, and should die on the cross and be raised again. The comparison ends there. It is these kinds of blended elements that rob the few truths of their power.

The second god is the moon, literally "our holy mother." This is a syncretistic mixing of the pagan idea of the moon as a deity with the Catholic conception of the Virgin Mary. The result for many Indians is a female deity which is identified with the moon. This concept of the moon reaches into many areas of life, controlling the time of planting and the cutting of trees for posts and lumber. When there is an eclipse a quarrel is going on between the sun and moon. One is striking the other. If they get very angry the world might come to an end. When the eclipse occurs the elders go to the church to pray for protection. The Chols and other tribes believe in a sun god and in a moon goddess, which is a feature showing continuity with the ancient Mayan pantheon of gods of the sky, seen as the moon, sun and the stars.

In addition to the sun and moon there are a multitude of subordinate deities, which can be either friendly or evil. Plants and animals have resident spirits. A god of abundance may appear in the form of a triple ear of corn or in an especially healthy animal. A friendly spirit named Wahun resides in a plant which is boiled to make a broth. This broth can cause one part of a cornfield to produce more corn. Other spirits may appear as children in the morning, youths during the day and old men at night. They ride horseback through the clouds. Lightning comes from these spirits to defend the villages.

The most dangerous evil spirit is named Ahal. Ahal is the spirit of the devil and is capable of appearing in many forms. It may appear as a woman who seduces men. When a victim sins with her, he turns into an animal and dies. There are a host of other evil spirits. Some inhabit caves, some approach lost travelers on the road in the form of a guide, only to lose their victims in the jungle. The evil spirit of the ground will attempt to capture the soul of a child who falls down, causing the child to become sick and die. Sacrifices must be made to this spirit to convince it to release the soul of the child.

It is believed that the spirits in the world move about freely like the wind and may attach themselves to an object or person. The belief is that spirits do not actually enter objects, but attach themselves to the object. They may not enter a person, but as with an object, they may attach themselves to the person. They are controlled by the great spirit, the sun. These spirits may be entreated and summoned by man. Appearances may be in a dream, a person, an animal or a ghost. One Indian reported seeing a spirit in the form of a dwarf in the shadow of a wooden cross. The figure danced, talked, sat down and leaned against the cross.

The Indians also believe in familiar spirits. It is believed by many who are caught up in the web of syncretism that an individual may have an alter ego, a second spirit, which attaches itself to him. It may be the spirit of an animal. If the animal corresponding to this spirit is killed or dies, the man with the spirit will die also. A man who has the spirit of an jaguar will say, "I am a jaguar." He will cover himself with a jaguar skin. An owl is thought to have a spirit which corresponds to the spirit of a man because it cries at night. A small mountain cat or a dog may also have this relationship to humans.

This superstitious dependence on a pantheon of gods first creates sickness, and then dogs the spirit, sometimes to death.

The people are the casualties. It affects not just their spiritual but also their physical being, making life doubly difficult, full of fear and hopelessness. As Aulie reports, "Sickness dogs the step of every Indian family. Very few enjoy good health. Infant mortality is high. Babies are delivered by midwives who know nothing of asepsis. It is a common occurrence for the newborn child to be infected with tetanus and die in a week or ten days. Those who do survive infancy struggle through a period of malnutrition and parasitic infection when weaned." It is held that sickness is caused by spirit activity and that the condition is relieved by appeasing the spirit which caused it.

The shaman is the only doctor many ever know. He is called when one is sick. When he arrives he examines the sick person and tells him his reason for being sick. He then sends someone to buy liquor for a liquor massage, telling the sick person's family that he also needs a chicken, a turkey, a duck or a pig. He sacrifices the animal and with herbs applies the blood of the dead animal to the patient's face, hands and feet. He mixes the blood with the liquor and the sick man drinks it. The shaman drinks some of the liquor, but also blows part of it out upon the sick person. If he doesn't get well the shaman, in a no-lose situation, says that someone has caused the sickness. He then takes the wrist of the sick man, but rather than taking his pulse, he divines what enemy caused the sickness and tells him who the enemy is. Sometimes the accused person is summoned. The Shaman, in front of the sick person, will accost the other person by accusing him of causing the sickness and telling him he must now remove it. The accused will reply, " I will." He then repeats the shaman's ritual, so that the person might get well. But if he does not obey the shaman, the father of the sick may strike him or even kill the person accused of causing the sickness.

Aulie quotes Thomas Gage, not a Spaniard but a European in the 1600's, almost a hundred years after Cortez took control of the places of worship, explaining how the roots of syncretism had been planted by Cortez and his priests, syncretistic rituals that still have a very strong hold today. Gage wrote:

> As for their religion they (the Indians) are outwardly such as the Spaniards but inwardly hard to believe that which is above sense, nature, and the visible sight of the eyes, and many of them to this day do incline to worship idols of rocks and stones and are given to much superstition, and to observe cross wares, and meeting of beasts in them, the flying of birds, their appearing and singing near their houses at such and such times. Many are given to witchcraft, and are deluded by the devil to believe that their life depends upon the life of such a beast (which they take unto them as their familiar spirit) and think that when that beast dies they must die, when he is chased, their hearts pant, when he is faint they faint; nay it happened that by the devil's delusion they appear in the shape of that beast, which is commonly by their choice, a Buck, or Doe, a Lion , or Tiger, or Dog, or Eagle. . . they yield unto the Popish Religion, especially to the worshipping of the Saint's images, because they look upon them as much like unto their forefather's idols; and secondly because they see some of them painted with Beasts as Hierom with a Lion, Anthony with an Ass, and other wild beasts, Dominick with a Dog, Blas with a Hog, Mark with a Bull, and John with an Eagle, they are more confirmed in their delusions, and think verily those Saints were of their opinion and that those beasts were their familiar spirits in whose shape they also were trans-

formed when they lived, and with whom they died. All Indians are much affected unto these Popish saints."

Aulie goes on to write, "This. . . of which Gage writes. . .persists in spite of 450 years of contact with Christianity and western civilization. This is the belief that a human being may have an alter ego in certain animal forms." It should be emphasized that this belief still continues today.

Another historian's words are still a warning to us today. John Leddy Phelan wrote, "The Spaniard attempted to do too much. . . to make the Indians Spaniards as well as Christians. The Spaniards were running the very real danger of failing in both endeavors."

In the end, the cross of Syncretism, which is Christopaganism, replaces the very heart of Christianity with its teaching that since God is far off, He left the oversight of the world to the saints who were visualized and worshiped as images that replaced the pre-Columbian idols. They turned from stone idols to images made of wood and plaster with Christian names, which then too became a fusion of Christian and pagan elements with their own spiritual power, enslaving the people to paganism and superstition. The fear and the hopelessness remain.

Contemporary Christopaganism has evolved to include Secularism, in which those searching for meaning, in an attempt to fill their spiritual vacuum, borrow from the naturalistic explanation of all of existence. Rationalism and materialism become the new gods.

From this have come demoralization, revolution, alcoholism, suicides - today's Chiapas.

The city of Ochue is a graphic modern illustration of how syncretism controls the life of a village. The villager's patron saint is St. Thomas. Every spring there are pilgrimages to burn candles and to pray to him for rain. They worship him by having a good time, i.e. getting drunk on posh, the sacred drink.

On their way to the fiesta they stop at a large sacred cave where the spirits dwell. They have a time of prayer and worship to the earth's spirits. They then move into the city, where an announcement is made that St. Thomas is alive, and ready to bring rain. The fiesta then begins.

Older men sit around and tell the children the story of St. Thomas, as it has been passed down from generation to generation. It is the story of how St. Thomas delivered the people from the wrathful god of heaven.

There was a time when the great god of heaven did not like the smell of the people of this village, so he created a new race who did not sweat nor have excrement, so they smelled good. This great god wanted to destroy all Txsotils and replace them with good-smelling people. St. Thomas heard about this and when the great god was not watching, he killed all of the race that god had created to replace the "smelly ones." Then Thomas, having some second thoughts, came down to earth. He found a mule, loaded with candles, bottles of posh, and sky rockets. He lit the candles, drank the posh, got appropriately drunk, and shot the rockets into the sky as a peace offering to the god of heaven.

The god of heaven then discovered that all his new race were dead and he was very angry. When the gifts of celebration, prayers and rockets were seen in heaven, he forgave them and no god has tried to kill them since, thanks to our saint, Thomas. Jesus comes into the picture only vaguely. These people still believe today that St. Thomas is their Savior.

Not everyone, though, has been robotized by the imposed beliefs of syncretic paganism. Two teenagers were more than skeptical about all the beliefs that controlled every part of their existence, from the time they awoke until the time they went to sleep at night, from the time they were old enough to think for themselves, until they were finally taught that the church would do their thinking for them and that they must simply be obedient to the the many gods or suffer the consequences. The priest had preached many times about the saints that surrounded their sanctuary as being "alive", watching over their lives, protecting them, while at the same time punishing them. They watched as peasants bought candles to burn at the saints feet, or put in the offering boxes money that literally took food from the mouths of their children.

Carefully laying their plans to, for once and all, test the words of their padre, they hid themselves behind the altar, and waited.

Most of the candles turned to smudges of wax on the dirt floor as they waited. Many of the people had gone to their homes, but others huddled under blankets in the city square until tomorrow, when they would buy more candles, drink more posh, and say more prayers. The two boys carefully lit a small candle and made their way to the feet of one of most important saints.

Stepping with their bare feet on wax on the floor, one took out a knife. As one held up the candle to the feet of the saint, the other took the knife and cut a gash in the top of the saint's foot. Surely, they thought, if St. Thomas is alive and we cut his foot, he will bleed. Frightened, shaking with the realization of what they were about to do, their resolve became firm as they saw that if this saint were alive, he bled plaster-of-Paris. They had their answer. They had been lied to. These were plaster saints. As they talked about it, their disenchantment grew. They were ready to tell their parents, but first they needed more proof that what the padre had been telling them, or at least part of it, was not true.

Another warning that they had always heard, since they could understand the padre's words, was that if anyone dared to touch the offering box, they would be severely punished by God. The boys knew that this sacred box, containing the offerings and money from the required candle purchases was what fed much of the priest's power over the people. Again, they hid behind the altar and waited until the doors were locked before carefully striking a match and lighting their candle. This time instead of a knife, they had a large screw driver. It took several hours, but they finally broke the lock on the offering box. They knew that one of the first things that was done each morning was to empty it. Now they knew why. It was almost full of pesos, which they would later call "blood money greater than the thirty pieces of silver Judas had received for his betrayal of Christ." They only took a part of the money so that the padre would not know that it had been broken into. They planned to secretly return the next day what they took. They didn't want to be thieves as well. They went back to the altar, crawled back into their hiding place, ready to quietly escape as soon as the first door was open in the morning, and before the offerings were collected. It was a night that changed their lives. The saints didn't bleed for the church, the people did. The saints didn't answer their prayers, no one did. They knew that a real God who heard prayers, if He really existed, would bleed, and would not take from the poor and give to the rich, but would help to feed the hungry and clothe the naked.

Their risky test was a vast step into what for them was the unknown, but they were willing to pay whatever price they must to find the truth about the spiritually enslaving sword of syncretism.

Syncretism is a very heavy cross. It is sometimes so weighty that those under it cannot get off their knees. Regretfully, there are no Roman soldiers around to order someone else to carry it for them.

———— ✳ ————

The clamor of barking dogs disrupted the quiet approach of early morning, awaking Pasquala. She shivered on her blanket as the dirt floor reached through it with icy fingers. It wasn't so much the chill of early morning that made her shiver, but the nightmares. They were back. Maybe they never left; she couldn't remember.

Last night she had dreamt about her father. Though his face was hidden under his hat and she never saw his eyes, she knew it was him him. She could smell that bitter pungency of his body, mixed with the sweet, venomous scent of the posh. He was running through a never-ending cornfield, stumbling as he fled deeper and deeper into the stalks. Something was pursuing him. She could not see a body or a face, but it was there behind her father, closing in on him. It passed like some invisible tide pursuing the terrified man, bending and breaking the corn stalks, the precious ears of corn falling to the ground to rot. On and on he ran, head bobbing up and down before this flood of death. One faltering step, one instant of sobriety, one glance within himself, and he would be swallowed by the darkness of reality. Clearly, his time had run out.

Pasquala hated him, even as she cried for him. Her mother was there in the dream as well. While the darkness chased her father into eternity, her mother sat on the ground before a cross of candles. Her face was hidden too, pressed against the earth, as she cried out to the forces of the spirit world. The candles were melting, wavering in the blackness. The wax turned to blood as it flowed across the dirt, and her mother shuddered like the flames. One by one, they flickered out. A presence was there, strengthened with each extinguished light. An evil. Then a scream, ripping through the dark, ripping through her heart, ripping her awake. It had been her own.

And so she lay there shivering, listening to the snarling dogs, sweating in the cold.

A year had passed since the bus ride, since the hot lands, since her mother died. Pasquala and her younger sisters had returned again to San Juan Chamula. Rosa lived here, their older sister who stayed behind with her husband when her mother took the others to the fields to work. Rosa took them to see the governor of Chamula, who allowed them to have a deserted one room shack on the edge of town, and the hect-acre of land that it was built on.

It was lonely. Pasquala had lived thirteen years now, and had two younger sisters to keep alive. It wasn't the work she struggled with. Her back was already conditioned and bent from the Jefe's fields, and the little girls helped pull weeds and plant seeds in the dirt behind their shack. Work was actually the easiest thing about living alone. But at night, when the phantoms played with the window latch, and the nightmares crawled about in her mind, she longed to curl up in the warmth of her mother's breast and be soothed by her strength.

Now she must be the strong one, for though she was still a little girl, it was she her sisters clung to when the terror of the night bit them.

She stood, and wrapped her wool skirt around herself. Rosa would be here soon. Her older sister had given birth to six children since the time they left for the hot lands, but the first three died as infants. That was not uncommon among Indian women. Many of them gave birth seven or eight times, but only had two or three children to show for it. Yajval Balamil often claimed their lives before they reached maturity, especially in families that were not wealthy enough to afford frequent sac-rifices, or who could not contribute much to the fiestas. Rosa was proud of her young son and her two daughters. Pasquala was the only person she trusted to mind them on days when Rosa went into town to sell things to the tourists, or into the field to help her husband. In exchange for the help, Rosa would quietly slip Pasquala and her sisters some extra tortillas or a dish of cornmeal, without her husband's knowledge. He would never let Rosa pay someone to help her, not even her own sister.

By the time Pasquala had walked down the path to the well for water and back she could hear Rosa's voice.

"Rosa!" she cried excitedly, hurrying the last few steps of the path. Her skin tingled from the warmth of the rising sun, and from the joy of company after the desertion of the long night.

"Good morning, sister," returned Rosa. Pasquala noticed that her eyes held more than the usual fear. A mother always felt fear, for she must always be watchful that her child did not fall into the disfavor of the spirits. Each time one of her children stumbled and fell to the ground, as all children must, the soul fell into the hands of Yajval Balamil, and would remain there until a candle was burned and prayers were said to intercede for it. For this reason, a mother made frequent trips to the church, always guarding her children against the reaches of evil.

"Are you going to San Cristobal today, sister?" Pasquala did not ask about the fear behind her eyes.

"Gustavo is sick." She didn't need to say more. Pasquala felt her fear now. Gustavo was the oldest. He was the only boy. He was the first survivor after Rosa's three dead children. He had been unable to eat for five days now. Rosa had been burning candles daily, and even left the fields to go to the church to pray, but he wasn't getting better. Heat rose off his skin, so that one could feel it without even making contact. Even a thin mixture of corn meal and water would send his stomach into convulsions of vomiting and diarrhea.

"I'm taking him to the healer," she said flatly.

"To Aunt Marta?" Pasquala tasted the fear on her tongue, remembering the time she had visited Marta the healer.

"No, she is gone to gather herbs in the mountains. I will go to Agustino." Her mouth was dry, even as she said his name. Agustino was a powerful healer. Some said he had seen the face of Yajval Balamil, while in a trance. Agustino cost a lot of money.

Pasquala could not meet her sister's eyes. She knew what she would see. She knew the hope was gone, and that this next thing must now be done. Gustavo was near death; only a sacrifice would save him. Even then one was never sure, for the wills of the spirits were not often kind.

"I will burn a candle for you, my sister," she whispered, and turned to enter the shack before she dropped the water pail in her hand.

"Pasquala."

She stopped and turned, trembling.

"If Gustavo does not live. . ." A tear hung on the high edge of her cheekbone, then fell down her dark skin. "If he does not live, I cannot bear it." She turned and left before the thought could fall into meaning, leaving silence in her wake.

The sun moved slowly that day. Pasquala tried to use her hands, and not her mind. As she worked to break the land in time for planting, the ache of her muscles provided little distraction from her screaming thoughts. Each time she lifted the iron hoe towards the sky, it was anger that arched her back, yet it was fear that made the blade shudder each time she tore into the roots and rocks, dulling the strength of the blow. Her sisters followed behind her, pulling weeds and throwing the smaller rocks off into the underbrush at the clearing's edge. They too muttered prayers beneath their breath, for even eight years out of the womb is enough time to know the power of the spirits and the fear of death.

They paused in mid-afternoon for their main meal, but only sat staring at the corn and pepper salsa, while the flies lost their timidity and walked untouched through the food. No one spoke. Afterwards, they left the field and sat outside the door, watching the path for Rosa's return.

For two hours they sat.

Finally, the youngest dared to break the silence. "Will Gustavo die, Pasquala?" she asked timidly, as though knowing the answer but unable to swallow the question any longer.

"No!" Pasquala answered sharply. Angrily.

"Agustino is a powerful man. His voice will be heard by the spirits. He will know what to do."

That was all. No more words were spoken as the shadows climbed out of the trees and strangled the remaining daylight. In the distance, Pasquala heard the fading chatter of the women washing clothes in the creek, as they scattered to their houses to fix dinner for their husbands.

An aching pain, like fingers around Pasquala's skull, made it difficult to breathe. Sometimes, she wished she could stop breathing. Simply stop pulling in and pushing out air. Her small chest felt so heavy some days that she was sure she was too tired to lift it one more time. If thirteen years had exhausted her this much, she dreaded to think how she would feel after another thirteen. But she feared death too much to truly wish for it. And even if she could have the luxury of escaping the burden of her own life, her younger sisters couldn't survive yet without her, and she knew it.

These were the thoughts that fought through her mind as she sat under the sun's coils, waiting for Rosa to reappear. Sweat bubbled on her skin, then melted in the heat, bonding her embroidered blouse to her back. She tried to send her mind to other places, but where else was one to go? Even an imagination required the hope of something different, and this young girl was too much a captive to reality to dream of anything different. Tonight would hold the same dreams, of the same phantoms, that carried the same fear. Tomorrow would be the same sun, and the same stubborn ground, with the same pain at the bottom of her back, and the same choking heartbeat in her chest.

What was it like to drown? It couldn't feel much different than this. The weight of a thousand feet standing on your stomach, wrenching the breath from your lungs, and wringing out the strength of every muscle. Your eyeballs aching in your head, threatening to burst, while your throat gagged on fright, but had no voice.

Can a mind so small feel despair this great? One does not have to live too long to know the suffocation of hopelessness. Life is generous that way, and the razor's edge of suffering cuts young and old alike.

Gustavo would not live. The thought did not surprise her, grieve her, or even anger her. It simply fell with a heavy thud into the bottom of her chest. All the blood of San Juan Chamula could not quench the spirit's thirst for death; how could a chicken compare to the taste of a human soul? It was a riddle, a joke, a comic tragedy. They were simply slaves to the whims of the spirit world, guided in their delusion by powerless healers and powerful priests. She wanted to vomit, to empty her stomach of nausea and her mind from thought.

She didn't want to wait anymore. She didn't want to hear the wails of Rosa as she shuffled through the dust towards her house. She didn't want to see death in her eyes, or taste the tears of the phantom's triumph. She couldn't bear lying in bed, while her young sisters clung to her own empty shell, weeping for reassurance that she could no longer create. She had enough, too much, more than she could bear, and she fell on the ground in her agony. Her face lay on the dirt of the earth that bound her, and tears no longer came.

Then there was light. A voice. A cry. A laugh. A laugh? She lay there and listened, sure that the trees were only mocking her pain and rejoicing in her anguish. But it was there again. Laughter winging through the sky that spun above her, reviving the pulse in her veins. Some mirage of sound that dared her to believe in it, to hold on to itself, to taste its joy.

It was Gustavo. Flying over the stony path with naked feet, dancing free from the clutches of death. Alive, exploding with aliveness, and defying death, he leapt into her arms and covered her cry with kisses. He leapt from her arms and danced on the head of despair, waving his arms to the fading sky with all the exuberance of youth.

Rosa followed him, sprinting from the tree line, crying, gasping and laughing, babbling in that nonsensical language of euphoria. A weeping Pasquala, a living Gustavo, a delirious Rosa and two younger sisters fell into a heap of celebration, and even the gathering night seemed to leave them untouched. As the party untangled themselves, no words were spoken. There was no speech for this moment. How does one use words to express a victory over death? And so they were content to let embraces and tears and laughter sing their song of freedom.

Finally, they moved into the tiny house, to eat and hear Rosa tell her tale. Pasquala shut the door and windows tightly, for no phantoms must steal their joy this evening. The weakness of death's certainty was still within her, and she sat on the floor clinging to Gustavo while her sister pounded kernels of corn into meal. The mad delirium of their joy glazed the surface of her thoughts, but seeds of fear still lived within her belly.

"Tell me Rosa. Tell me how it happened. Tell me how Gustavo lives tonight." She had to know, though she was terrified to learn the price. Yet everything seemed different this time. Never had she seen a child healed so quickly, or so completely. And often the happiness of healing was shadowed by the reality of the cost. The village healers might intercede to save a life, but only in exchange for a debt that could never be repaid. Pasquala remembered the time she herself was taken to the healer. Even in unconsciousness she had been disturbed, and remembered feeling more oppressed than freed. No, healings were not usually things of joy, but were instead surrounded with a heaviness that couldn't be explained.

Rosa sat to serve the food, struggling to capture the ocean of emotion in the net of language. She felt like music. Not the sounds of music, or the desire for song, but like the music itself. Like the spirit of some song that lifted up and filled the air with an eternal expression of movement, like her body could evaporate into some harmony that would crush tears from the coldest heart, and steal breath from the strongest lungs.

Nothing in all of life compared to this feeling. This must be freedom.

"Rosa, tell us," pled Pasquala, but her sister was somewhere else. There was something burning in her eyes, a hidden secret she was thriving on. Pasquala sensed it.

Pushing her pile of tortillas towards her newly resurrected son, Rosa hesitated, searching for the words. It was all so mysterious. So unexplainable. So ridiculous, and yet so impossibly wonderful. She found her breath, and lunged into the story.

Rosa could scarcely remember the walk from Pasquala's hut on the edge of the village to Agustino's house. She only remembered the weight of her dying son in her arms, pulling her down towards the rocky ground. The muscles in her shoulders were cut with knives of exhaustion, but the pain in her shoulders, the rocks that stabbed her bare feet and the weight of her child were buried and overshadowed by the mountain of grief that crushed her breath and stole her strength. Why must the gods take the only gift they had ever given her? She had nothing more than her children. All of the world that she knew spun behind their bright eyes and unquestioning faith in her. The hunger in their bellies drove each step of her three hour walk to market each week. The light of their laughter numbed the pain of her own misery each day. The warmth of their bodies pressed against hers comforted her when the phantoms crept in her dreams at night.

Now the lust of the spirits demanded the soul of her child, and she was driven to kneel to their desires. She tripped on the path, and Gustavo moaned in her arms. She gripped his sweating body in her strong arms, refusing to let him fall into the open mouth of the world beyond. The great bellows of despair blew coals of anger into a fire that burned her throat and singed the edges of her mind. Was there no justice? She did not deserve this! No one had been more faithful to worship, no one contributed more to the fiestas honoring the gods, no one prayed more faithfully to appease the whims of the spirit world. Were the gods deaf and blind, that they could not hear and see her desperate devotion?

Would there ever be enough blood to quench their thirst and bring peace?

All of these things Rosa thought as she struggled along the way to Agustino's doorstep. Agustino the healer. Agustino the intercessor. Agustino, her only hope.

She fell to the dirt at his door, still clutching the boy in her arms. Tears choked her voice, and Rosa collapsed against the door. She remembered Agustino's face close to hers, and saw his mouth moving in some silent speech. He must have been talking, but all Rosa could hear was the rushing of wings beating inside her head. She held Gustavo tighter, her arms locked in the rigor mortis that death's certainty brings. Suddenly Agustino was the enemy, a communicator with the spirit world, a conspirator against everything good. She tried to cry out a warning, a prayer. . .she begged him for mercy.

Then all was quiet. For an instant. Rosa felt his hand on her face, gentle and tender. She lay in the eye of the storm, and found Agustino's eyes.

"Please. Help me. My son, his soul is close to death. I will pay you. I will pay you whatever you ask. You must shed blood and appease the will of Yajval Balamil. Please! Please." Agustino took the dying body of the boy and the dying heart of the mother into his arms. He did not reach for his ceremonial knife. He did not scan the yard for a chicken soul, he did not calculate a price, he did not conjure up the fire. He simply took them in his arms and bathed them with his tears. For many minutes he wept, and the three held each other on the brink of death.

Then he spoke. "Mother." It was a term of respect. It was not spoken with the usual arrogance a healer held the right to, but spoken softly, as a village man might speak to his elder.

"Mother," he began again, for this was a difficult road he meant to walk. "I cannot make the sacrifice for the soul of your son." A simple statement. Rosa didn't move. Her mind slipped off the edge of reason and into an anesthetic of delirium. She couldn't argue, her tongue had turned to clay. It was treason. He had broken the unspoken code of their humanity. Agustino was the appointed one, around whom the circle of intercession revolved. He was the voice of the people in the underworld, the intercessor who pled their cases before the impulses of the gods. He was the healer, the high priest, and the keeper of the highest duty. They were slaves to the demands of the spirits, and the healer alone could bring them mercy. Yet he was refusing. And by his refusal, he brought her son death.

All this she absorbed in silence, unable to cry out.

Through the numbness of silence, the healer's voice reached her again.

"I am no longer a servant of Yajval Balamil; I worship another God. He is called Jehovah-Rafa, 'the One who Heals.'"

The final blasphemy. She lay still on the dirt and felt her son in her arms, waiting for the spirits to take their lives. But all was still. The rushing sound of phantom wings fell silent, and fear seemed to cower at the healer's confession. Rosa waited for death to strike them, for the pain of her soul's destruction, but instead she felt some foreign and frightening power of peace. Her mind tried to condemn this feeling, to return to the fear she knew so intimately, yet instead she felt a salty thirst spread into her heart. Parched and dry, she let the words penetrate its calloused walls.

Agustino sensed the thirsty soil of her heart, and poured out onto it his living water.

"Mother, it is written in a book. This book holds the stories of our ancestors, how they lived from the beginning of time. For many generations this book has been lost in other lands, and we have been blind to the knowledge of our ancestors. We have been living our lives according to the directions of our priests and healers. We have raised our children to believe in and fear the things that we ourselves did not understand. But now I have seen this book and heard the stories, and in them I have witnessed the truth."

Agustino paused, for his emotion was great. To think that this book had been hidden for so long, while his people struggled in darkness, was so unfair. The stories of his father's fathers had been written long ago, and yet Agustino and his people had not known any of them.

Rosa felt the last breaths of her son's life beneath her hands. The dirt floor had swallowed each of her tears where they fell, and her eyes were empty of any more.

Agustino told her the story of the beginning of men as it was written in the book. Before the earliest ancestors lived on the earth, there was a great Creator God. The great Creator God built the mountains with his fingertips, and commanded the sun with his voice. He flung the stars into their place in the sky, and lightning and thunder answered his call. He was greater than all the other gods of the earth, and everything was in the control of this Creator God.

It was the Creator God who made humans. He designed the form of their bodies, and the intricacies of their minds. He gave them the power to run and to speak, and allowed them to make choices of their own will. The Creator God had great love for these first ancestors and they were His companions.

Rosa lay still in the awe of it. One God who was greater than all other gods? Greater than the spirits, the shamans, the healers. . . greater than Yajval Balamil? And this God had love for humans? Though this was a beautiful story, surely it couldn't be true. Yet in her disbelief, the flies and the late afternoon heat fed on her with little disruption, so tightly was her attention fixed on this fantasy.

Agustino told her of the earliest ancestors. They too disobeyed the wishes of the Creator God, and lived in fear of His punishment. The Creator God demanded blood payments for unfaithfulness, and in exchange for these blood payments Creator God would have mercy on the humans who disobeyed Him. The early ancestors made continual sacrifices, offering sheep, goats, and birds to substitute for their own souls. But as the Creator God accepted these blood payments, it gave Him great sadness. He knew that for all of time, there would not be enough blood on the earth to cover the unfaithfulness of His human companions.

In all of Rosa's weakened, desperate state, she recognized this story. It was her own story. Like her ancestors, she lived in fear of the spirits; the dying child in her arms was proof of their unquenchable thirst for blood. This Jehovah-Rafa was no different. Perhaps He loved the human race, maybe He had power over the other gods, but He still held humans in an unpayable debt of retribution for their unfaithfulness.

But Agustino was still speaking. He spoke of the Jehovah God's sadness at the state of His people. The people feared him, while He desired only their love. So the Creator God did a thing that could never be understood. Creator God had one Son. He loved this only Son with such a great love, it was as if the son were part of Himself. They were equals, Father and Son. Agustino cast a glance upon the mother still trembling in his arms. She understood this love between a parent and an only son. Her own son lay scorched by the heat from his own body, ready to fall through that narrow barrier that separates this life from the next, and yet his mother held him back by the will of her own heart. Mother Rosa knew the love between the Creator God and His only Son.

He told her how the Creator God sent His only Son to earth, where He walked in the dirt beside their ancestors. The Son of the Creator God became a human, and felt the pain that humans feel. He was perfect, and held all the power that his Father the Creator God had. This Son they called Jehovah-Rafa, because He had power to heal. He gave sight to a blind man, simply by touching him with His hands. He made crippled people walk by speaking a word, and made sick children well with His voice. This Healing One could command phantoms and spirits to leave the nightmares of villagers, and the spirits would obey him.

But the Creator God had a greater plan for His Son. The humans on earth, Rosa's ancestors, took this Son of the Creator God and killed Him. Though the Son Jehovah had done no wrong thing, and never once needed to offer a blood payment for unfaithfulness, it was the Creator God's plan that His Son would be the final blood payment for all of humankind. It was as if the Creator God sacrificed Himself to pay the blood payment for His human companions. This was to show how great His love was for His human children.

Tears lit the darkness of Rosa's eyes. For a moment, even the condition of her own son was forgotten, so absorbed was she in the story of this Creator God who offered His own lifeblood to rescue His human children from their bondage to blood payments. It was unimaginable. Not one of the gods she worshiped would do a thing like this. No, their demand for blood was ever increasing and their reward was not life, but the death of her own child. She could not understand why a god would choose this path. And why did this Jehovah-Rafa, this healing

God with power over other gods, over sickness, over night-mares. . . why did He have to die?

For the first time she spoke, from the dimness of the shadowed hut floor. "Why?"

Agustino cried as well. He did not understand why. He understood the need for blood payments. He understood the power of this Creator God. But while he did not understand this Love, he believed it must be true. This light of Truth burned within him and seared the wetness in his eyes. His heart and stomach tangled as one, surging beneath his ribs like a fish returned to freedom in a bottomless river of water.

He answered her. There was more. This story did not end in the whirlpool of heat and blood and screaming of countless other sacrifices. This story did not end with the ghosts of spirit breath stirring candle flames and chicken feathers while gravity pulled the candle fires into earthbound darkness. There was more. The lifeblood of Creator God spilled out, and the great sacrifice was completed. But the power of the transaction was greater than the power of death. The Son of the Creator God went into a grave of death, but in three days, He came out alive! Alive! Living! He proved His power over blindness, over phantoms, over darkness, and now He proved that He was greater even than death. As the villagers in San Juan Chamula beg the spirits for mercy, the Creator God lives on forever. As Rosa begs Yajval Balamil for life, the One Who Heals is still alive!

His words came gently, urgently, as rivers often flood. Not crashing over the banks in a muddy torrent, but simply filling ever fuller, until they rise over every boundary, every tree, every phantom, and every fear. Rosa was drowning in their meaning. She could not breathe a contradiction. All the protests of six thousand years in darkness were swallowed by the hope this story told.

She believed. She believed! Certainty ran like rain into her desert soul. Every pore of dry decrepit darkness was invaded with the waterlight of truth. Dark webbed wings of phantom fears once perched securely on the branches of her mind now thundered in a panicked frenzy, fleeing from the rising tide of freedom. Deep rooted parasites of doubt and firmly planted spirits of despair fled from the swinging sword of new belief. She was drenched in life, and gripped in the fingers of a new Master who held authority over all the rest.

It was a fantasy. Too suddenly. Too easily. Buried for so many generations, Truth had finally penetrated this corner of the continent and it was outrageous in its claim. It was a reality.

Rosa had not spoken a word, but Agustino watched the encasing of darkness dissolve in her eyes. His joy was great. He joined a hundred million angels in heaven, shouting for joy and worshipping the Creator God for healing the blindness of another human child. He felt that barrier between the seen and unseen quiver in the tremor of their dancing feet, thundering to all of eternity in a fiesta that would daunt all others.

Rosa and Agustino fought to contain all the explosion of joy that heaven ignited within the fragile brick walls of this village hut. Outside, the chickens cackled in the yard, and women bundled up their wash from the bottom of the putrid creek, unaware that light had penetrated the darkness. Spirits stirred angrily about the transformation, confused by this disturbance in their stronghold. Their clamor broke through Gustavo's sweating unconscious, and he moaned a plea from the door of death.

Rosa asked Agustino the question he had anticipated. "Can Jehovah-Rafa heal my son?"

He looked far into the new light behind her eyes. "Yes." He had no doubt.

The boy lay on the dirt, still in his mother's grip. He appeared to be shrinking from Agustino's countenance. Moaning, he tossed his arm weakly towards his burning forehead. Fear rippled the sweat on his face, as forces beyond tugged at his life-strength. Gustavo had not eaten for days, and his cheek bones protruded from below his eyes like some skeleton hiding in a shroud of dark skin.

Agustino took the boy in his arms. He felt the presence of the spirit world infesting the limp body, like vultures feeding on a carrion soul. Like Abraham carrying Isaac to the altar in his arms, Agustino held the boy before the throne of heaven. He looked up, past the dry straw of his roof, past the green awning of trees, past the cloud ceiling of heaven and fixed his eyes on the face of a Creator God he now recognized. Agustino spoke to the Healer. In the ancient staccato speech of the Tzotzil people, he spoke to the God of his ancestors.

"Creator God." He could say nothing more. Hidden cisterns of tears shattered and poured over his upturned eyes, cut his cheeks, pooled in his throat and choked his words. The presence of the Creator God suffocated him with awe. He was speaking to the God above all gods, and this God was listening. Mouthing the name of the boy with the lips of his heart, Agustino lay Gustavo in the Maker's gaze. He knew no incantation was needed. No eloquence would impress the Writer of speech. Agustino the village healer let the ache in his spirit plead the request.

Gustavo's frame twitched in agony. Rosa placed her hands on his head and felt the furious oven within. The temperature climbed.

Again Agustino lifted his eyes. and whispered in reverence. "Jehovah. Your children are here at your feet. You are the great Creator God. You are the God above all other gods. Spare the life of your child Gustavo. . ." He could get no further aloud. Shuddering, he implored for mercy, for life out of death.

Still the boy lay. His breathing lifted his chest in small transparent convulsions. Up. Down. Up. Down. The thin white shirt stuck to his chest in a camouflage of dirt and sweat that matched the pale fragility of his skin. Forehead and cheeks fought in a mask of tension, belying the battle beneath.

Agustino placed his hands over Rosa's and together they cradled the head of the child.

"Jehovah-Rafa. You are the God who heals. There is no power, no spirit, no sickness, and no death that is greater than you Jehovah-Rafa. . ." In all earnestness and humility of a poor man before the Highest God, he cried, "Accept the blood of your only son in place of the soul of this boy."

It was finished. He sobbed in the realization of this request, in the magnitude of the sacrifice. He forgot the boy, the mother, the heat wavering in the hut and the nausea in his stomach. He saw a tree, with a man stretched across its branches and held there with nails of iron. Falling on the ground at the feet of the man, he felt warm blood on his neck, on his shoulders, running down his back. Another one's blood. A sacrifice, yet there was no noise. No screaming, no smell of death. . . only warmth. Tears fell from the man on the tree, and splashed in the bloodstream, and he heard the sound of crying. Weeping, mingled with his own. He bathed in the tears, filling his mouth with the taste of their anguish. Peace. He felt peace.

A voice shattered the vision, and though the man on the tree faded away, the taste of peace still steeped in his throat and warmed his chest.

"Mama." The boy sat up, as if awakening from a dream.

"Mama."

He lived.

For the second time in that hour, the angels swirled about in a dance of euphoria, a dance of homage to their Master. Their voices could be heard across the eternity of space, like wind across leaves, water over water, like the harmony of all the ocean's deepness. . . "Great and marvelous are your deeds, Lord God Almighty!"

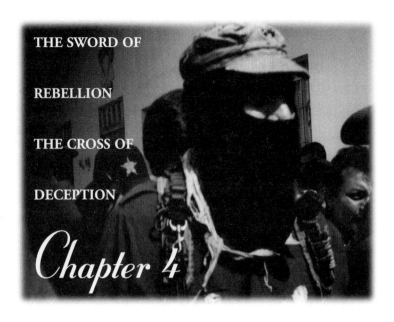

THE SWORD OF

REBELLION

THE CROSS OF

DECEPTION

Chapter 4

> *. . . Utter a parable to the rebellious house, and say to them,*
> *Thus says the Lord God:*
> *" Put on a pot . . . and also pour water into it.*
> *. . . Fill it with choice cuts; take the choice of the flock.*
> *Also pile fuel bones under it, make it boil well,*
> *and let the cuts simmer in it.*
> *. . .Woe to the bloody city, to the pot whose scum is in it,*
> *And whose scum is not gone from it!*
> *Bring it out piece by piece, on which no lot has fallen.*
> *For her blood is in her midst; she set it on top of a rock;*
> *She did not pour it on the ground, to cover it with dust. . .*
> *Woe to the bloody city! I too will make the pyre great.*
> *Heap on the wood, kindle the fire;*
> *Cook the meat well, mix in the spices,*
> *and let the cuts be burned up.*
> *Then set the pot empty on the coals,*

That it may become hot and its bronze may burn,
That its filthiness may be melted in it,
that its scum may be consumed.
She has wearied herself with lies,
and her great scum has not gone from her.
. . . Because I have purged you, and you were not purged,
you will not be purged of your filthiness anymore,
till I have caused My fury to rest upon you.
I, the Lord, have spoken it; it shall come to pass, and I
will do it; I will not hold back. . .
According to your ways and according to your deeds
they will judge you," says the Lord God.
Ezekiel 24:3-14

THE SWORD OF REBELLION

Many swords are double-edged, cutting in both directions. Such are the swords of revolution and rebellion.

Webster defines revolution as "a sudden, radical change; the overthrow of one government or ruler and the substitution of another by the governed, creating a radical change," and rebellion as "open, armed, and usually unsuccessful defiance or resistance to an established government." Based on these definitions, one has to say that Mexico's last revolution was in 1910 and its last rebellion began on the eve of New Year's Day, 1994, in the state of Chiapas.

The first hints of the 1994 uprising came from the village of Ocosingo, 65 miles from San Cristobal. There were reports that small groups of a revolutionary organization named the EZLN, but commonly referred to as the Zapatistas, were hijacking trucks. Later, the hijackings would be recognized as a clever diversionary tactic. Ocosingo was a town with a reputation for trouble. It appeared to the army general in charge of the area that a group of hoodlums in a small village were chasing some "religious fanatics" who refused to take part in the New Year's fiesta. The general assured his staff that he had taken care of the problem. He sent extra soldiers to make sure nothing happened that would need to be reported to his superiors in the capital of Tuxtla. Though there was a deluge of people moving into the neighboring villages of Las Margaritas, Altamirane and Chanal, they were mostly women bringing in wares to sell to New Year's Eve revelers, and young boys eager for a celebration, nothing that demanded their attention. Most importantly, San Cristobal was as quiet as could be expected on New Year's Eve.

As the general and his staff went home to celebrate with their wives and friends, it went unnoticed that several busses and trucks outside San Cristobal were hijacked. The confusion and excitement in the air was attributed to young people beginning their celebration early. The military laughed it off and continued their own celebrations.

What the military did not notice was the number of Indians coming to San Cristobal for the celebration. Had they set up military checkpoints, they would have noticed that the huge, blanket-wrapped bundles the women carried on their heads and the old pieces of luggage carried by old men and children were not filled with the usual fruits and vegetables, chickens, and liquor for the celebration, but with guns and machetes.

Young men wearing traditional black pants, white shirts and baseball caps were sliding off the backs of trucks, and making their way up alleys to meeting places at warehouses and homes. Their clothes were exchanged for green slacks, brown shirts, and a red neck scarf. Some took butcher's knives and tied them to the ends of long sticks. Others had wooden guns, painted with black shoe polish to look like the real thing.

As darkness fell and the celebrations intensified, the word came, and the young men headed for the city sewers, dry at this time of year. The sewer lines led them to the center of town, and when the signal was given, they streamed up out of the manholes, ready to set aright the historic injustices against their people.

Near the plaza square, another group of men donned black pants and sweaters, red scarves and black ski masks. They were the leaders of this assault. They wore two red stars above their sweater pockets. A few drunks slept in the plaza. The circular restaurant in its center, which only hours before had blared music through loudspeakers was now dark, its doors barred.

One by one, the young rebels appeared from every direction, moving toward the plaza, walking, singing, shouting:

"Long live the Mexican Revolution!"
"Long live the Zapatista National Army!"
"Long live the Indian People in arms!"

Those residents and tourists not passed out or sleeping rolled over in bed, assuming they were hearing a band of late revelers. Weapons shot into the air sounded like firecrackers. The advance guard stormed the Municipal Building, breaking doors and windows. Before the city realized what was really happening, the young army, with their hand-made bayonets and wooden guns, ransacked the offices, hauling files, furniture, and wall hangings into the plaza to burn them.

Local and out of state reporters in town had received anonymous phone calls earlier, and began arriving on the scene at about four a.m. The army commanders slept on, as sporadic fighting continued on in the outskirts of town.

In the city plaza, an older Indian in his fifties appeared, wearing an old straw hat and the signature red scarf, surrounded by fellow Indian chieftains. He signaled the press that he had something to say. A reporter from the local newspaper, the El Tiempo, knew who he was and spread the world to fellow correspondents. He was Comandante "El Felipe," an Zapatista leader. Comandante El Felipe pulled a piece of paper from his pocket and began to read slowly and haltingly, betraying his semi-literacy. Reporters and a few tourists awakened by all the noise listened as he read in Spanish:

"We have come to San Cristobal to do a revolution. We have fought peacefully for years, trying to get a solution by the government that has never cared to solve our long problem about land rights and other problems."

Without waiting for questions, he pulled from his other pocket a well-used and tattered pamphlet. In halting Spanish, he read, "This declaration of war on the federal army of Mexico, the basic army of the dictatorship we suffer under, led by the party in power and headed by the executive power today is in the hands of a maximum illegitimate leader, Carlos Salian de Fortare. Our object," he shouted, "is to march to the capital of the country, freeing every city along the way." Then as a side remark, as though suddenly prompted by his fellow leaders, "and of course we will have free elections."

The press raced each other to the few available telephones. Others headed for the internet. Within hours, planes loaded with journalists from around the world arrived at the capital city of Tuxtla, 90 miles away. After renting anything with four wheels, they rushed to cover what was then thought to be the biggest revolution in Mexico since 1910. Their by-line had already been written for them, and they would send by satellite their pictures of a rag-tag army of young kids in green slacks and brown shirts, wielding wooden guns, whose leaders were dressed all in black, with ski masks and brown hats.

This revolution would not produce much for the Indians, but it would produce an image who was larger than life. Across the plaza, a young former college professor from Mexico City disembarked from a hijacked Volkswagon. He too, wore a ski mask, but was armed with a walkie-talkie and the first up-to-date weapon on the scene. Two masked women followed him, handing out weapons. He began speaking to the media, and they listened. He was articulate, speaking both Spanish and English perfectly. He said he didn't want his picture taken because, "We want to remain anonymous so we will not become corrupted." Laughing, he added, "Well, those of us who are the most handsome must protect ourselves." Cameras recorded these images; satellites transmitted them around the world. The revolution died being born, but Subcomandante Marcos had just become larger than life.

Most of the physical fighting took place in the city of Ocosingo, where five hundred rebels took over the municipal palace. In the fighting, the head of the municipal police was killed, and the police force raised the white flag and surrendered.

The real and continuing battle, the public relations war, took place in San Cristobal.

In a few days, the physical fighting was over. One hundred and forty-five people were dead, and hundreds more wounded; there were over 25,000 war refugees. But it was not as much revolution as it was "rebellion as grand theatre." It would not go down as the greatest revolution in Mexico since 1910, but that didn't matter to some, because the story had successfully gone out to the world, and that which could not have been accomplished with machetes and wooden guns was instead accomplished by the mass media. The plaza in San Cristobal is again filled with tourists, though the Zapatistas still threaten. There have been numerous peace talks, but no agreement of any substance, leaving the question:

What was the rebellion really about?

Helen and Samuel Hoffman have served for nearly 40 years as Reformed Church in America missionaries among the Txeltal and Tojolobal people of Chiapas. Samuel Hoffman describes what has happened there as being like a chess game:

"Having played some chess helps one to understand what happened at the start of 1994 in Chiapas, Mexico. What we saw was a complicated game of political chess.

In Mexico, the PRI political party has been in power since 1929. The PAN party has challenged it from the right side for years, but it has not been able to widen its support base. However, in the past few years a stronger challenge has come from the left, although that challenge has been weakened by the fractioning and disunity of the various parties on the left.

In the 1988 national election, Cuauhtemoc Cardenas broke from the PRI party and made a strong run for the presidency, supported by disenchanted PRI people and some of the parties on the left. For the first time in history, the PRI party looked vulnerable.

In the 1994 election year, the chess pieces were being moved again. The goal, of course, was for each side to eliminate as many of an opponent's pieces as possible and finally to capture his king.

Now, to expose your opponent's big pieces, one needs to sacrifice some pawns of his own. That is where the Zapatistas came in. For years the political left has been preparing the lowland Indians for their sacrificial role. Political Catholic priests, catechists, and layworkers organized the remote villages into unions 'so that they would have a political voice with which to talk with the government, and an organization that could help them in the development of their area.'

Slowly these unions were turned to an anti-government stance. The Indians were told that the rich landowners were their enemies, and that they were poor because others were rich. They were told that the government had abandoned them to poverty and misery. Eventually they were told that the only way for them to receive what they deserved would be to arm themselves, declare war on the government, and to take from the rich what was rightfully theirs. Professional guerrilla organizers arrived. They distributed arms and communication equipment and gave the Indians some military training.

The Indians accepted their role as pawns. On New Year's weekend last January, they came out of the lowlands and occupied several municipal centers. They even marched out boldly to attack the army base near San Cristobal de Las Casas, and they were sacrificed there by their leaders. Others remained in Ocosingo to challenge the advancing Mexican army. Many more Zapatista pawns were killed there before they retreated toward the lowlands.

But the sacrifice of the pawns was quite successful in the sense that the PRI sustained some losses. The PRI ex-governor of Chiapas, Patrocinio Gonzales Garrido, who had become the Secretary of the President of Mexico, and his replacement in Chiapas, Governor Elmar Setzer M. both became casualties. They were asked to resign and take responsibility for the embarrassing uprising of the Zapatistas.

The opposition hoped for an even greater outcome: the disruption of the national elections in August or the defeat of the PRI presidential candidate. They also hoped that the Mexican military would over-react, and that the bombing of villages and the many human rights violations would bring them increased sympathy and support, and that the wave of righteous indignation would result in further casualties among the government leaders.

But the President of Mexico made a move which surprised the opponents. He declared a quick cease-fire, offered amnesty to the Zapatistas, and sent a respected government leader to seek for a peaceful solution. This caught the Zapatista leaders by surprise, and some confusion and delays followed as they had to switch from the expected battle of bullets in the jungle to the battle of words at the negotiating table.

In the meantime, an intense effort was made by the Zapatistas to interpret the events to the world in a manner that benefited their side. The Zapatistas and their sympathetic press supports pictured the rebels as humble heroes who only demanded justice, democracy and equality.

Meanwhile, the government told of all its efforts to help the people of the area, promising a rapid response to their problems and needs. They announced an ambitious program of road improvements throughout the area.

At the same time, human rights organizations sent representatives immediately following the uprising to monitor the fighting and to investigate accusations against the federal military forces.

In the background are the people who got hurt in the fallout: Mexican and Indian cattle ranchers, whose ranches were plundered and whose cattle are being consumed by the Zapatistas; also 15,000 refugees from the lowland villages who fled. They were afraid of getting caught in a cross-fire between the army and Zapatistas; or they abandoned their homes after being given the option by the Zapatistas of joining them, leaving, or being killed.

So what has happened in Chiapas this year has been a messy political game, with lots of people getting hurt. But in politics, as in chess, the ones who move the pieces sacrifice them for their ultimate goals. And when the game is over, the winners receive their political prizes, and the pieces are put away and forgotten about - until it is time for another game."

The Rebels

Where there is a "rebellion", there must be "rebels."

The major anti-government antagonist in this newly spawned rebellion, in a land with a long history of such upheavals, is a group officially known as the Zapatista National Liberation Front (EZLN), so named after one of Mexico's preeminent revolutionary heroes, Emilio Zapata.

Zapata was a brilliant young leader, a mestizo peasant who, at the age of 30, played a leading role in the Mexican Revolution of the early 1900's, supporting a cause similar to that of the EZLN: helping the Indians regain their "sacred lands." Zapata was known and respected for his honesty, courage and fervor for justice for the Indians. It was a time when land, mostly communal or church owned, was made available for purchase only to wealthy private parties. This automatically excluded the Indians. Some of the Indians protested, and were either killed or exiled as slaves to Yucatan.

The President at that time, Jose Marie Morales, was generally outspoken in favor of the Indians, but he secretly sided with the wealthy hacienda owners, being more concerned about politics than justice.

Zapata created enemies in high places by attempting to lead an Indian revolt. There were several attempts on his life, and he went into hiding when the government offered a ransom for his life. In April of 1919, Zapata was informed that a high ranking military officer wanted to defect to his revolutionary forces. The military even had several of their own officer's aids killed to add credence to their story. Zapata, after considerable discussion with his own people, agreed in good faith to meet the officer and accept his government sword. A place and time were set for the meeting. Zapata and his troops were ambushed and killed as they rode out to meet the defecting officer. Every April a wreath is laid at the feet of the statue of Zapata in Cualta. The wreath, like the promises of most presidents since, quickly wilts and is blown away by the winds of continued injustice.

This brief piece of history is not meant to infer that Marcos is another Zapata, but rather that the problem of Zapata's time is still the problem today: political injustice surrounding the central issue of land ownership and use.

The EZLN had its genesis on November 16, 1983, when six idealists from Mexico City arrived in Chiapas to join forces with dissident peasants. They began a movement that immediately went underground to plan a rebellion through military and political action.

The leader of the new movement was a well known Mexican Marxist revolutionary who went by the name of Commander-In-Chief German. His real name is Fernando Yanez. He is the brother of a well known Mexican Marxist dissident, Cesar German Yanez, known popularly among leftists as "El Hermano Pedro," who was killed in 1973 during a clash in Chiapas when a defector betrayed his whereabouts to the military.

German, like many of the Marxists in Mexico, was a product of the "coffee shop Marxists" in the Mexican University system. Though they called themselves revolutionaries, in the end they proved only to be rebels, creating a disturbance, but accomplishing little of significance.

Though it may have appeared to outside observers that the Zapatistas were an "Indian Army," they were actually far from it. They have always been a well organized and well financed white-Marxist guerrilla group, based in Mexico City. Though their initial communiques preached only justice for the Indians, theirs was in reality a call for a Socialist struggle in its most radical form.

Their official documents were as hard-line as any among Latin America's Marxist rebel groups. Kept from the press was one which read, "The National Liberation Forces fight against Imperialist ideology by challenging it with the science of history and society: Marxism-Leninism, which has demonstrated its validity in all triumphant revolutions of this century. That is why, in addition to fighting against the ideological domain of capitalism, we also fight against those who, infiltrated in the labor and peasant movement and within the leftist movement, renege on the revolutionary essence of Marxism and promote reformist ideals and collaboration among the classes, instead of fighting to death for the exploited against the oppressors."

Shortly after the January 1 uprising, Sub-Comandante Marcos, the new spokesman for the EZLN, began down-playing all calls for any kind of a class struggle. He stripped his communiques of anything sounding like "class warfare" or other traditional Marxist jargon. At a Peace Conference in San Cristobal, he spoke of "Injustice" and "Indian rights," and used other similar terms to trigger a positive reaction from the press. At the same time, however, the most prevalent pieces of literature being read by his associates were those of Che Guevera, Fidel Castro's partner in the Cuban Revolution.

The reason for Marcos' emphasis on the Indian nature of the rebellion was obvious: his Zapatista advisers, including Chiapa's Roman Catholic Church Bishop Samuel Ruiz, and rebel sympathizers in Europe and the United States, were advising him that Marxism was no longer a popular issue, but an "Indian Rebellion" theme would have media and financial support.

It worked! Many leftist intellectuals around the world, still smarting from the failure of Communism in Russia and Eastern Europe, and having given up on Fidel Castro, hailed this as the first post-communist leftist rebel movement.

There is another perspective of the rebellion and the rebels, however, that one will not hear from the popular media. Samuel Hoffman points out several misconceptions about the situation in Chiapas:

"Myth Number One: 'It was a spontaneous revolt of oppressed indigenous tribes.'

The truth is that these indigenous groups have been organized, oriented, armed, and trained during the past fifteen years by the Roman Catholic Church and left-wing political organizers.

Myth Number Two: 'This revolt has been initiated and

led by rural Mayan Indians.'

The truth is that the leadership is from the outside, that is, Mexican (mestizo) and foreign priests and political organizers, of whom Sub-Comandante Marcos is an example. The Tzeltal and Tojolabal Indians are pawns being sacrificed by these left-wing political leaders, who hope to influence the national elections in August.

Myth Number Three: 'The Zapatistas are landless peasants whose land has been taken over by wealthy, powerful cattle ranchers.'

The truth is that most of the Zapatistas come from lowland villages established on national land during the past thirty years, in which each family was given forty acres of land by the government. During the past fifty years, the Indians of Chiapas have not lost any land to mestizo ranchers. Quite the opposite. As their population has increased, the Indians have purchased some land from the ranchers and have been given much land by the government. At present, the Zapatistas and other Indians emboldened by their success have taken over, ransacked, or are squatting on many ranches. The great majority of these ranches are small family ranches of less than 200 acres.

Myth Number Four: 'The Zapatistas timed their revolt to coincide with the inauguration of the NAFTA (North American Free Trade Agreement), to emphasize their opposition to it.'

Actually the Indians of the lowlands in Chiapas are not aware of and will be little affected by NAFTA. Their proclaimed opposition to it shows how much they are being used by the left-wing political leaders, who have the defeat of NAFTA as part of their political agenda.

Myth Number Five: 'The Zapatista revolt was a desperate attempt to force the government to respond to their needs and grievances. It was their only alternative, as the government has been completely unresponsive to them.'

Although unfulfilled promises, mismanagement, inefficiency, and graft have hurt the government's programs in Chiapas, yet much progress has been made in education, roads, electrification, water, and health in rural Chiapas, including the Zapatista area.

Myth Number Six: 'The government and the army have been guilty of widespread human rights abuses against the Zapatistas.'

There were incidences of abuse by the army. However, the President's immediate declaration of a cease-fire and amnesty stopped the violence. As in all revolts and wars, there have been human rights violations on both sides.

Myth Number Seven: 'Human rights organizations have been very influential and impartial in monitoring and limiting human rights violations in Chiapas.'

These organizations have helped limit army abuses and have kept the government from vigorously responding to the Zapatista threat and to their invasion of properties. However, the human rights organizations are selective about whose rights they protect. They have ignored Zapatista abuses, and the suffering of the Indians in the Zapatista areas who have not joined the movement.

Myth Number Eight: 'Bishop Samuel Ruiz of San Cristobal should be a candidate fore the Nobel Peace Prize for his role as mediator in the conflict.'

Bishop Samuel Ruiz is directly responsible for this conflict. His embracing of Liberation Theology twenty years
ago and his demand that his priests become politically
active laid the foundation for the Zapatista movement.
The Zapatistas requested that he be the mediator, knowing that he would be a strong advocate for their side. The
government accepted his nomination, feeling that since
he had caused the mess, he should help clean it up."

Rebel Number One - Sub-Comandante Marcos

Real weapons were shooting real bullets, and people were
dying in towns like Ocosingo, Las Margaritas, Chanal and
Altamierano, but the real fighting was taking place in the city
plaza in San Cristobal, in the shadows of the Bishop's cathedral
and the government center. The weapons were not toy guns, but
video cameras. There were no missiles fired into distant targets,
but rather, words hurled at the speed of sound by satellites to the
news capitals of the world. Those who had spent years preparing
for this opportunity remembered the effectiveness of the reports
filed by one correspondent in Cuba and distributed around the
world by the New York Times. These reports presented Castro as
a true revolutionary with one goal: to free the people of Cuba
from oppression.

The EZLN's plan was to place Mexico City into a no-win situation. If the national army moved in to suppress the revolt, pictures would be transmitted live around the world of a modern day
army, equipped by the United States, massacring an army of kids
with wooden guns. If the Army did not stop the revolt and exercise the authority of the government, the revolution would spread
like it did in 1910.

Appearing in the plaza on that first day of 1994 was a tall
man dressed in black clothing and a ski mask, carrying a machine
gun and a walkie talkie. He began to talk to the press in perfect
Spanish and English. The fact that the message of a "Indian upris-

ing" was being explained by a tall, white-skinned mestizo seemed of little consequence to the press.

"Today we say enough is enough!" said Marcos. "To the people of Mexico . . . We are the product of 500 years of struggle . . . they don't care that we have nothing, absolutely nothing, not even a roof over our heads: no land, no work, no health care, no food, no education. Nor are we able to freely and democratically elect our political representatives, nor is there independence from foreigners, nor is there peace or justice for ourselves and our children. But today, we say ENOUGH IS ENOUGH!"

A legend was born that day. He called himself Sub-Comandante Marcos. He spoke in poetic language about the poverty and injustice under which the Indians had lived for over 500 years. He demanded land for the poor. It made a nice sound byte, and the world ate it up, especially those intelligencia who felt alone and isolated now that Marxist dictators were no longer in fashion. Weren't all Marxist ideals on the scrap heap of history? Dare they hope? Yes, at least for a short time.

Marcos was a different kind of rebel. He had a sense of humor that resonated with the press. Here was a man who was dead serious, but affable. He was no egotistical, inept Daniel Ortega, or overly zealous Che Guevera, but an "ordinary guy," albeit, one with a machine gun and an army. He did not fit the traditional image of a Marxist rebel leader. When asked by a woman tourist in the city plaza at the height of the "revolt" why he wore a ski mask, he told her to the press' glee, "Only the most handsome of us are required to wear them, for our own protection." A Swiss couple were concerned that their air-conditioned tourist bus would not be allowed to leave town to visit the Mayan Culture ruins at Palenque. Marcos wrote out a safe-conduct pass, and handing it to them said, "Sorry for the inconvenience, but this is a revolution."

He was asked why so many of his soldiers were 14-year-old kids. His reply was, "You grow up fast in the jungle." "Why did some of the rebels fight with only with sharpened sticks and machetes?" Sub-Comandante Marcos said his goal was not to kill or be killed but to make themselves heard. "White people," he said, "only listen to the Indians if they have a gun in their hand."

When the questions got personal he answered with a joke. If someone asked if he had been in San Francisco, he said, "Yes, why not?" He said he became a revolutionary because his folks "had a bad divorce." He played the press like a musical instrument, and much of the world sang along.

How do you speak such good English? "Because like many Mexicans I sneaked across the border to work in the United States." Without prompting, he jokingly told them he had held a job blowing up rubber dolls in a sex shop in San Francisco, driven a taxi in New Orleans, worked as a security guard for the Dallas Cowboy's cheerleaders, and taught skiing in Aspen, Colorado. "That's where I get my ski masks," he joked. And for the record, for all those teenagers writing the letters, "I'm single." Was this the truth or was he leading them on? Did it even really matter? Then, perhaps, but not now.

In the days after the initial uprising, the Mexican army drove the Zapatistas out of San Cristobal and surrounded the jungle stronghold where Marcos took refuge. Over one hundred soldiers, rebels, and civilians had been killed, but Marcos survived.

Marcos mania swept a nation that was hungry for an honest-to- goodness hero they could share with the world. The assassination of a presidential candidate and a chief of police in Tijuana had created a need for some good news, and Marcos was that man. Mexico City, which had a long flirting relationship with Marxist rebels, rose to its feet and erupted in cries of "Viva Marcos." Thousands took to the streets to protest the government crackdown on the rebels. For some years Indian children had come to San Cristobal to sell miniature home-made dolls. Now they added a ski mask and a tiny, crudely made wooden gun to the doll's hands and sold them as souvenirs, along with Marcos T-shirts, key chains and even underwear emblazoned with Marcos' image.

Eventually, the press and the public began to get tired of his jokes and insincerity. They started packing their video cameras and laptops and headed for the airport as his glow faded. His credibility as a serious leader began to dissolve when negotiations with the government over issues such as land for the Indians and democratic reform dragged on without results. Marcos' real agenda couldn't withstand that kind of scrutiny. Some Zapatistas supporters were angry that Marcos had rejected a government peace proposal. Some grew tired of his jokes, or thought he took too much attention for himself, or didn't think he knew what he wanted.

Some members of the press anointed him, however, as he continued to hide behind his mask. Ed Bradley of CBS's Sixty Minutes did a live interview from Marcos' hide-out, which was so "well-hidden" that Bradley and his camera crew had no trouble finding him, introducing him to millions around the world by saying, "What Robin Hood was to the people of Sherwood Forest, Subcomandante Marcos has become to the people of Mexico - a fighter for the rights of peasants who are trapped in poverty by large landowners."

Behind his ski mask, one couldn't tell if he was grinning when he told Bradley, "We want democracy, I mean, the right for the people to choose the government and way of this government. We want liberty, I mean, every people has the right to choose one way or another way. We want justice."

Bradley intoned, with a straight, serious face, "So basically, what it is you're asking for are basic individual rights."

Marcos responded with an affirmative, "Yes."

Bradley added, "What we call in the United States, 'Life, liberty and the pursuit of happiness?'"

From Marcos, another affirmative "Yes."

What Bradley did not tell the Sixty Minutes listeners was that Marcos' Indian army was in reality the armed wing of a white-dominated Marxist guerrilla group operating out of Mexico City, headed by Commander in Chief Germain. The press continued their infatuation, and Marcos answered every question with a smile and poetic eloquence.

A correspondent from the Miami Herald, Andres Oppenheimer, was not so easily fooled. After interviewing Marcos, he wrote, "Judging from the Zapatista's initial communiques, internal rebel documents, and Marcos' own response when I asked him about this, there is little doubt that the Zapatistas grew up as a traditional Marxist guerrilla group which changed its rhetoric after the January 1 rebellion, when its media-savvy leader discovered the advantages of playing up the Indian participation in his uprising - the one aspect of this revolution that captured the world's imagination."

But who is this masked man that came to free the Indians? Is he actually an Indian?

Sub-Comandante Marcos has been identified by former associates as Rafael Guillen, one of eight children raised in a middle-class neighborhood in the coastal town of Tampice. His father owns a furniture store. Marcos was once a professor of graphic design at the Autonomous Metropolitan University, a university known not so much for its graphic arts, but for its leftist politics. Marcos has been identified by people who have known him for a long period of time as a "hardline Marxist Guerrilla," and is far from being the "post-modern socialist" depicted by the press and the leftist intelligencia.

With his growing loss of public support, caused by his inability to bring about meaningful change, the government decided to try to arrest him. He fled into the jungle, where he remains today, but not before firing off one last joke. The government had printed for distribution a photograph of him without his mask. He said that it was not a picture of him, and, "the government was just trying to ruin my relations with women."

He has reappeared several times. He was given amnesty for peace negotiations held in San Cristobal. These negotiations accomplished very little and he returned to his jungle camp.

In 1998, five months had passed with no word from Marcos. Rumors were rampant. He was dying of malaria; he had been captured by the Guatemalan Army; he had taken his mask off and gone to France to watch the World Cup soccer championship.

Then in July, like a second-coming, this message was faxed to news organizations: "Yepa, yepa, yepa! Andale, andale! Arriba, arriba! Yepa, yepa!" It had Marcos' signature and neatly printed below were the words: Speedy Gonzalez. It shed little light on any of his plans for the Zapatistas. The speculations as to what he really meant to say were many. Poet and activist Homero Aridjis said, "At first I thought it was just a joke. Then I figured it could be something like a children's fable with a moral lesson. . . I came to believe it was a message in code to certain groups in Mexico, though I'm not sure what the message is supposed to mean."

A shorter message signed by Marcos was sent in Nahuatl, the language of the Aztecs which is still spoken in parts of central Mexico, but not in Chiapas. Some experts believe it was in the language of Emilieo Zapata, the spiritual father of the Zapatista movement. The message read, "Zapata lives. Your father is here. He is not dead yet."

The Mexican newspaper who predicted the January 1994 rebellion suggested it might be a code to his followers, as a prelude to increased rebel activity in Chiapas.

On the other hand, it may have only been Marcos' innate ability to make news, as the week the message was released was the week President Zedillo toured Chiapas. A week later a visit was planned by U.N. Secretary General Kofi Annan. Marcos wants people to know he is still a force to be reckoned with.

One thing not hidden behind any mask is that Marcos has rewritten the rules for rebellion in the electronic age. Rebellions usually place a call for armed insurrection, but Marcos simply uses the threat of violence and the sheer force of his personality to draw attention to his cause through the mass media and a vast E-mail network. Marcos, like no one since Zapata, brought to the forefront the nearly intolerable injustices heaped upon the Indians and the heavy cross they carry each day. However, there are still no signs of peace or solutions to the injustice; no revolution, no "radical change." There is only rebellion, only "unsuccessful defiance." Marcos remains in his jungle hide-out, writing poetry, remaining a media mystery figure.

Rebel Number Two - Bishop Samuel Ruiz

"Ah, yes. . ," she smiles as she crosses herself, "He is truly a saint. I pray to him every day." A few food stalls away a young man spits out, "A devil, that is what he is, a devil hiding behind a cossack, that is why he is called the red Bishop." The person they are both referring to is Bishop Samuel Ruiz Garcia, Bishop of Chiapas, and known to many as Don Samuel. Some say he thrives on controversy, and he wouldn't want it any other way.

In 1960, Pope John XXIII consecrated Samuel Ruiz Garcia as the bishop of Chiapas at the age of 35, the office once held by San Cristobal himself. Thirty-eight years later, his lined face fringed with sparse, gray hair, and his shoulders slightly stooped, he still carries a look of determination. Although he may have changed physically he remains the same ideologically.

He shrugs off the reported thirty assassination attempts, but is thoughtful when speaking about the Indians and his Church. "We must realize," he tells other bishops, "the Catholic Church oppressed the Indians from the beginning. And after 500 years there is not one country in Latin America with an autonomous church." Little wonder that at the behest of the Pope in October 1993, the Vatican Envoy to Mexico City asked him to retire. He refused, intending his appointment to last his lifetime.

Today he supervises 88 priests and 7,000 indigenous lay workers in the three main ethnic groups in Chiapas. There are no ethnic priests, for they refuse to take a vow of celibacy. It is believed that in recent years he has played a large role in the daily work of the EZLN. He does not openly participate himself. Most of his work comes through his priests, and their doctrine of Liberation Theology. Andres Oppenheimer, in his book Bordering On Chaos, writes: "Under the leadership of militant bishop Ruiz, the Roman Catholic diocese of San Cristobal de las Casas had organized up to four thousand lay workers to help spread the gospel of liberation theology among Chiapas Indian communities. It is difficult to separate the EZLN from liberation theologians."

Oppenheimer continues, "The (Indians) are being taught to build a new society in the unpopulated lands of the Lacandon jungle. Catholic Church steered-communities had been thriving in the jungle for years, with their priest and lay workers preaching resistance, against the government."

As for the EZLN, Oppenheimer says, "Over the years they infiltrated militant Roman Catholic peasant groups created by San Cristobal de las Cases Bishop, Ruiz, the activist priest whom right-wing Chiapas ranchers call 'the Red Bishop'."[1]

After observing the January revolt, a missionary who had lived most of his adult life in Chiapas, echoed this belief as he wrote the following:

"What is rarely included in the news is the relationship of Roman Catholic bishop Samuel Ruiz to this uprising. It is significant that the uprising is limited to the diocese of bishop Ruiz. The Zapatista Army is made up of unions that were organized under the bishop's supervision. They have been reinforced and led by Central American Guerrillas."

The bishop has covered his tracks well, however, and he has many friends and admirers. He recently was honored by a human rights organization in Washington D.C. for his advocacy of human rights for the indigenous people of Chiapas. He and the two other Roman Catholic bishops of Chiapas have offered their services to mediate between the Zapatistas and the Mexican government. The government is under pressure from the human rights organizations to accept the offer." (Now an accomplished fact.)

But many of the people of Chiapas are scornfully indignant about the bishop's offer, and they place the blame for the uprising on bishop Samuel Ruiz. As an elderly friend said to me this week, 'The Bishop throws a stone, and then he hides his hand.'

One reporter began his report in LA PRENSE, a Mexico City Newspaper dated January 4, 1994, with these words, 'The hands of the government are tied. It can do nothing to nullify the actions of the person it considers to be the principal promoter of the violence that has bloodied the diocese of San Cristobal de Las Cases in Chiapas: the Catholic Bishop Samuel Ruiz.'

The bishop denies any relationship to the Zapatista Army of National Liberation. He also denies that he ever has encouraged any violence. It may be that the movement has raced out of his control. But it definitely was the bishop who planted and watered the tree that is giving the harvest of violence and death in Chiapas today."

It may be possible to separate the bishop from the Zapatistas, but not from Liberation Theology. The bishop's top aid, in an interview talking about the bishop's decision to add his considerable support and leadership to the Liberation Theology movement, called it on two occasions "his conversion." The bishop, now certainly cheated out of two thing in life he wanted: a Nobel Peace Prize and a Red Cardinal's hat, may now have to settle for something less. There are reports that he is raising money to build a Cathedral in Chiapas that will rival St. Peters in Rome, becoming the Vatican of the West.

The Bishop, using obvious symbolism, has been know to ride into Indian villages on the back of a donkey. Therefore, it is important to take a brief look at that entry of our Lord Jesus Christ into Jerusalem, noting that the only true parallel between Christ's entry and that of Bishop Ruiz is the donkey.

The day we now know as Palm Sunday was the day on which Jewish families would enter Jerusalem to choose the lamb that was to be slain in their place at Passover, so that spiritual death would pass over them. Jesus entered the city on a donkey that day, offering Himself as the Lamb of God, the ultimate and final blood sacrifice to take away the sins of the world, and fulfilling Zechariah's prophecy that God's just and humble Messiah King would arrive on a donkey, bringing salvation to the world.

This was also the day that in the past, false messiahs had made grand entries down the Mount of Olives and up to the holy city, to declare themselves as the long-awaited Messiah, coming to free the Jews from Roman political rule. Rebels would then riot, bringing Roman garrisons who crushed the rioters. Little wonder that when Jesus came riding on a donkey in the manner of a king, tension resulted. Grim Roman soldiers stood with swords ready to slash the life from any rebellion before it became a threat to their power, as Herod had done after hearing of the Messiah's birth.

To the Jews, palm branches have symbolized longed for joy and salvation, but to the Romans, the palm branches symbolized rebellion. During the last successful Jewish revolt by the Maccabeans, Jewish coins were embossed with palm branches, a nationalistic symbol considered overtly political, having nothing to do with spiritual deliverance. The people were not shouting, "Hosanna, Son of the Most High God, our temple and our hearts are open to receive you. Come and deliver us from our sins." Rather, the shouts and palm branches were saying, "We cannot stand being oppressed by Roman injustice any longer. Come king, and free us! Deliver us. We want national deliverance!"

How did Jesus respond? He wept. He made no political speeches. No promises of an earthly kingdom of justice. He simply wept, tears running down His face as they did when He wept at Lazarus' grave. The people were as dead as Lazarus had been, but their future was without hope because they were not interested in a spiritual rebirth, or in gaining spiritual freedom. They were only interested in a national, political and cultural resurrection. They missed the whole point.

So has Bishop Ruiz. Jesus Christ has come to every village of Chiapas with the same message: "This is not about politics. This is about a Savior. Open your temple doors and the doors of your heart to me." He offers to each one His tears, tears shed over the hundreds of years that this land has suffered through spiritual death. Taste the salt of His tears. "Repent, for the Kingdom of God is at hand. I am your blood sacrifice. Choose Me."

Regretfully, there is a parallel between the crowds of Jerusalem and Chiapas. Jerusalem chose to crucify the True Revolutionary, and set free the rebel, Barabbas. Chiapas has put to death the real revolutionaries, those who have identified themselves with the Life of the Crucified Savior, while the rebels are set free to instigate more rebellion, and all the while injustice and wars continue.

How long, Oh Lord. How long?

But I fear, lest somehow, as the serpent deceived
Eve by his craftiness, so your minds may be corrupted
from the simplicity that is in Christ.

2 *Corinthians 11:3*

THE CROSS OF DECEPTION

Deception is a difficult cross to bear at any time, but especially when it is wrapped in a verbal cocoon of feigned righteous indignation.

During the 1960's, a Latin American theologian named Gustavo Gutierrez delivered a paper at a seminar on the theology of liberation. It was a time when many of the world's theologians were struggling with issues of faith, post-Enlightenment, skepticism and the supernatural in the natural world. While they were asking, "Where is God in an age of science and technology," the more practical Gutierrez was asking, "Where is the God of righteousness in a world of injustice, namely for the millions of poor in Latin America?" Pointing to the hovels of Latin America, the poor living in the shadow of wealth, Guiterrez struck a sympathetic chord when he stated unequivocally, "The starting point of Liberation Theology is a commitment to the poor." He was not speaking of the poor in spirit of Jesus' Beatitudes, but of the millions in Latin American churches living in sub-human conditions. His concern, rightfully so, was for the disenfranchised, those who had been marginalized to the very edges of society. It was a concern that was picked up by many well-meaning priests, who themselves had been bedeviled by the same problem. They took up the cry, "We are on the side of the poor, not because they are good, but because they are poor." Their argument was: "Christian theology must start from below, not from above." Christianity to them meant contending for the poor living on dirt floors without medicine or decent food. Their belief was that the poor of Latin America are the authentic theological source for understanding Christian thrust and practice.

This theology began in Europe when theologians were beginning a form of Christian thought that established religious inquiry on the basis of a norm other than the authority of tradition. The basic tenet of this theology was that the poor must be liberated from what they defined as "coercion by external control."

Liberation Theology grew out of the spirit of the Renaissance, an era of natural man with an insatiable quest for appreciation, idolization of the human spirit, and the celebration of freedom without restrictions. The spirit of the Renaissance sharply contrasted with the spirit of the Reformation. One lifted the spirit of man to assert his rebellious will, while the other recognized man's rebellion and God's grace to lead him to repentance and the forgiving authority of a loving God. Liberation Theology found its way to Latin America, but the Reformation did not.

Liberation Theology's perceived mission of the church is defined in terms of an historic struggle for liberation. They ascertained that theology does not just answer philosophical questions, but encompasses analysis, politics and economics. Theology becomes the second stage of Christianity, with feeding the poor being first. Actions come before words. They then set out to renovate the poor, believing that all of society, including the church, would follow and be renovated as well. Liberation Theology has but one doctrine: everything must center around the poor and the disenfranchised, a temporal base.

No one argues against justice for the poor being a part of Christianity's call to love. One cannot study the New Testament, walking with Jesus Christ across the Holy Land, without realizing that He had a tremendous love for the poor and disenfranchised. There is no question that to clothe the naked and feed the poor, to take care of widows and orphans is an integral part of our obeying God's Great Commandments.

Liberation Theology reached its apex in 1968, when Latin bishops placed on record, as part of the Medellin Document, that the Catholic church was no longer the defender of the eternal status quo. The church was now to take a stand for social reform and for "development through acts of conscience of the individual human being, namely the poor, the naked, the hungry and the widows - the disenfranchised who have been for too long moved to the farthest perimeters of human dignity."

At that time, however, it was impossible to separate such a movement from politics. Those were the days of the cold war, and the Soviets knew an open door for influence when they saw it. It was their own brand of good news when the Catholic church began offering a liberal democratic, yet reformist alternative to both the static, class-ridden, rigid "traditional Catholicism" in Latin America, and Marxism, with its certainty of a new, even more oppressive dictatorship of the proletariat. If Moscow believed in God they would have thought this was a marriage made in heaven. As Liberation Theology grew in popularity, Rome realized there would be no wedding, though there was some time of serious flirtation.

These events of history were too much of a burden for those who were going to build a new order of Christianity on the basis of Liberation Theology. In Nicaragua, the fall of Ortega and his Marxist-priest entourage was a prelude to the much greater crash in East Germany, where the people were "tearing down the wall." Marxism, though not totally discredited, had lost its tenure. The final knell was sounded more recently in Cuba when the Pope "put a cap on all the philosophical and theological confusion that entered into the hemisphere from the 1960's to the 1990's" - the socially correct, but theologically flawed Liberation Theology, thus ending any type of official support from the Roman Catholic Church.

One Cardinal in Rome told an American correspondent,

"The Latin Marxists were trying to mix up the theology of redemption with the theology of liberation, to make Christ the Redeemer into Christ the revolutionary, and to substitute the 'popular church' of the Marxists for the institutional church."

A good illustration of the political "hijacking" of Liberation Theology by the Marxist movement is the history of Daniel Ortega and the Sandinistas in Nicaragua. Liberation Theology was at its apex in Nicaragua when, to everyone's relief, Nicaragua's dictator, Anatasio Somazo was overthrown. He was replaced by Daniel Ortega. Ortega surrounded himself with a group of priests who were leaders in the Liberation Theology movement, and with sympathetic political leftists from Hollywood, New York and other centers of influence in the United States.

Four catholic priests held cabinet offices in Ortega's government. They spoke of Ortega's revolution as the "coming of the Kingdom of God." They were joined by leftist Protestant sympathizers from mainline U.S. denominations and high profile Hollywood personalities. One denominational leader in the United States declared, "It is required that we as Christians understand that biblical faith is inseparable from political militancy."

Ortega, in welcoming the Pope to Nicaragua, told the Pontiff at the airport, "Christians in Nicaragua (i.e.: Catholics) were basing themselves on faith corresponding to the (Marxist) revolution." The pope, who was then, and continues to be a strong opponent to Liberation Theology, was not amused.

The four catholic priests who had become cabinet members were later told by the pope to either leave Ortega's cabinet or the priesthood. They gave up their clerical collars, adding credence to the suspicion that they were not just "hijackers" of Liberation Theology, but disciples of Marxism. Their political statements in resigning from the priesthood were received with adoration outside Nicaragua, where demonstrators could go home at night and live a life far from the center of the storm.

One of Ortega's cabinet members said, "The only way to love

God, whom we do not see, is by contributing to the advancement of this revolutionary process in the most sensible and radical way possible. Only then shall we be loving our brothers whom we do see. Therefore, we say that to be a Christian is to be a revolutionary."

But what kind of a revolutionary? Fr. Ernesto Cardenal, Ortegas' Minister of Culture answered that question. "The only solution is Marxism," he said. "The revolution and the kingdom of heaven mentioned in the gospel are the same thing. A Christian should embrace Marxism if he wants to be with God and all men."

A revolutionary poster, one of many, trumpeted the message, "Faith without revolution is dead." On the cover of a popular and widely distributed pamphlet was a young man with a Che Guevera beret, a crucifix around his neck, an automatic rifle in one hand and molotov cocktail in the other. Inside were printed the words, "Jesus Christ is not enough for us." The Foreign Minister, Dr. Miguel D'Escota proclaimed, "One of the great blessings of the Church is Marxism."

The rallying cry of the liberation theologians, which spread from Nicaragua to neighboring countries was, "Christians won't be free without socialism, and socialism won't be built on the continent without Christians." The people of Nicaragua apparently didn't agree. The simple democratic process of free elections derailed Ortega and the liberation theologian's plans for the country and the rest of the continent. At the polls the people of Nicaragua sent Daniel Ortega and his fellow travelers packing, electing a new leader.

But is Marxist Liberation Theology really dead in Central America? Not in Chiapas, Mexico. Though the name may have been changed, the product is the same.

Twenty years ago, the bishop of San Cristobal de la Casas, Samuel Ruiz, invited Dominican priests from California, nuns from South Dakota, and Jesuits from Mexico City to go to the villages to stop the Protestant advance in the tribal area of the Tzeltal Indians.

One who lived there at the time reports that these Roman Catholic workers, who were not liberation theologians, followed the method previously used by the Protestants, of learning the indigenous language, encouraging the construction of chapels in every village, appointing lay leaders for each chapel, establishing an effective medical ministry, and encouraging the reading and study of the Bible.

Then something happened that would radically change the Church's focus on the local Indian tribes. The Bishop's Executive Secretary announced that Don Samuel, the bishop, was converted. To what? To Christ? To new Catholicism? No, to Liberation Theology.

After his discovery of Liberation Theology, the Bishop sent back the priests and nuns from California, South Dakota and Mexico City. He replaced them with seventy-five priests from his diocese, with the orders that their ministries had to include advocacy for the poor and involvement in their political struggle. In so doing, the Bishop effectively put Liberation Theology into practice in Southern Mexico. He issued an edict that any priest who did not want to be politically active should look for some other place to serve.

In a short period of time, language schools were forgotten. One priest is quoted as saying, "Let the Protestants study their Bibles, meanwhile, we will change the world." Catholic lay preachers focused on the Israelites' Exodus, encouraging the Indians to prepare to take over the private Mexican ranches in the valley, their land of Canaan. They chided those who hesitated, saying, "God wants to give you this land of Canaan, and you want to stay in bondage to Egypt?"

Guerrilla organizers arrived in the remote lowlands from Cuba, Guatemala and El Salvador. Rumors began to circulate about military activity, and the smuggling of arms, uniforms and communication equipment into the area. Strangers appeared in the villages carrying automatic rifles, beginning a campaign of intimidation against mestizo and Indian landowners, killing the owners and confiscating their land, all in the name of Liberation Theology. This action culminated on January 1, 1994, in San Cristobal de las Casas.

The primary problem with today's practice of Liberation Theology is well summarized by theologian and Seminary President Donald W. McCulloch, in his book The Trivialization of God, published by NavPress. He writes the following:

"The movement known as liberation theology has developed, in the last twenty years, into a more nuanced pattern of thought than its caricatures indicate. Without doubt, it has shed light on important streams in the biblical witness. But in its extremes it has often seemed more interested in the cause of liberating the oppressed than in trying to understand the God who liberates. It has tended to become captive to political and economic assumptions that have taken precedence over Scripture itself.

So Gustavo Gutierrez, one of the earliest and most influential liberation theologians, in his 'A Theology of Liberation,' reads the Exodus story as a paradigm for the struggle against oppression: "The liberation of Israel is a political action. . . Sent by Yahweh, Moses began a long, hard struggle for the liberation of his people. . . A gradual pedagogy of success and failures would be necessary for the Jewish people to become aware of the roots of their oppression, to struggle against it." The most sympathetic exegete to the cause of liberation may well question whether this is the point of the Exodus story. Is it really about the oppressed struggling against their oppressors? Or is it about a dramatic intervention of a liberating God who decided to save Israel? Lesslie Newgigin has pointed out that in much liberation theology Scripture functions only within the framework of a

Marxist interpretation of history, and that the real kernel of Scripture is seen to be whatever serves the cause of the oppressed. The irony is that "if the appeal is not to revelation as found in Scripture, but to the knowledge of human affairs which is available to observation and reason, a good case could be made for asserting that the poor are simply those who have failed in the struggle for existence and - in the interests of the race - will be eliminated by those who demonstrate their fitness to survive."

More is at stake here than hermeneutics. If God is brought in secondarily, after the problem (oppression) and solution (political and economic liberation) have been defined, that will invariably shape our image of God. We may view God, for example, as simply an aid to fulfilling our human aspirations, simply Big Help for what is essentially a human struggle for self-improvement.[2]

The evaluation of the Liberation Theology movement by the evangelicals in Chiapas is more to the point and less diplomatic. J. Paul Hoffman, seeing its genesis and watching its demise, wrote:

> "While the Mexican government talks about peace and negotiation, the Zapatista rebels in the Chiapas lowlands and their allied peasant organizations in the higher altitudes are expanding their areas of control. They are entering neutral villages and asking, 'Are you for the rich or are you for the poor?'
>
> If the villagers respond that they are for the poor, they are pressured to sign a document declaring that they are in support of the rebel movement. Last week one of the Tzeltal evangelicals in the village of Cuxulja responded, "I am not against either the rich or the poor. The Bible tells me that I should treat all people with respect and love." Because of his unwillingness to sign the document, the rebels chased him out of the village. He and his

family became a part of a new wave of Tzeltal refugees arriving in the town of Ocosingo.

This is the practical outcome of Liberation Theology's doctrine of God's preference for the poor. The reasoning goes like this:

In the world the rich oppress the poor.

God is against oppression.

Thus He is against the rich and for the poor.

Therefore, the church should also stand with the poor against the rich.

This seed has produced the violence and anarchy in Chiapas. During the past twenty years priests and cate-chists have spread the new doctrine, telling the Indians, 'All the land once belonged to your ancestors, but Spaniards and Mestizos stole it from them. You are poor and oppressed. As it was God's will that the Israelites take possession of the land of Canaan, so now it is God's will that you possess the land. Arm yourselves and take it!'

The result is that anyone who owns land has become a target for the invading groups. Hundreds of small fam-ily-owned ranches are being invaded, ranches that these families have developed during the past decades and in some cases for generations. Also, hundreds of Indians who have saved money and have purchased land from the ranchers are now among the 'rich Canaanites' who are being expelled from their land. Among those expelled from their land last week are two Tzeltal Indian widows and their children, who now are helpless refugees in Ocosingo.

Inspired by Liberation Theology, prompted by their own covetousness, and emboldened by the guns someone had provided them, seven months ago a dozen Indian families expelled the students and staff of the Tzeltal

Bible Center that had served the Tzeltal church as a leadership training center for thirty years.

There is something devilish about how Liberation Theology works. It begins with God's concern for the poor and then proceeds to legitimatize the armed invasion of the small farms owned by humble Mestizo and Indian families in Chiapas. It is commendable that certain Roman Catholic Church leaders are concerned about the poor. But there must be a better way of helping the poor than to tell them to steal from their neighbors.

In our sympathy toward the poor, we need to realize that one of the most harmful things we can do to them is to tell them that they are victims. Putting the blame for their poverty on someone else only will add to their demoralization. Telling them that the government, or the cattle rancher down the valley, or the storekeepers in town, or the authors of the NAFTA economic treaty are responsible for their poverty leaves them with no personal responsibility for their situation. We rob them of any initiative they have to improve their situation and of any motivation to change their negative and harmful lifestyles that have contributed to their poverty.

Telling the poor that they are poor because someone else is rich only plants hatred in their hearts. Further, such propaganda seems to justify their acts of violence and injustice.

I am not an expert in economics, but it seems to me that a false concept of wealth is widely held. This false concept declares that the world contains only a certain amount of wealth, and that if my neighbor has more than I do, he really has part of my share.

The truth is that wealth is not static. Wealth is created by productive work. As we say in colloquial American

English: we make money. So the goal of the government or of a political movement should not be the redistribution of the existing amount of wealth, that is, to take it from the rich and give it to the poor. Instead, the goal should be to create more wealth by promoting productive work, so that more wealth can be produced and shared.

The solution to rural poverty in Chiapas is not the invasion of productive family farms and the redistribution of their cattle and land. That only intensifies and universalizes the poverty. The solution is to help the poor peasants become more productive, so that additional wealth may be produced for them to share.

So what about God's preferential treatment of the poor? The Bible does speak clearly against the oppression of the poor by the wealthy and of workers by their employers. It encourages those who have, to share with those who have not. But it does not encourage class conflict and violent social upheaval to accomplish the redistribution of wealth.

The Bible urges God's people to care for the widows and orphans and foreigners in our communities. It goes on to point out the danger of being wealthy, since the pursuit of possessions so easily can replace our commitment to God. But it declares that the love of God is wide enough to include all people, including those who are wealthy. Prejudice or preferential treatment is not something that we can pin on God."

In 1977, another observer, Oscar Romero, a Roman Catholic Bishop added, "It would be worthless to have an economic liberation in which all the poor had their own house, their own money, but were all sinners, their hearts estranged from God. What good would that be? There are nations at present that are economically and socially quite advanced, for example those of northern Europe, and yet how much vice and excess."

"Liberation that raises a cry against others," writes the martyred Bishop, "is not true liberation. Liberation that means a revolution of hate and violence and takes away the lives of others or debases the dignity of others cannot be true liberty. True liberty does violence to self and, like Christ, who disregarded that He was sovereign, becomes a slave to serve others."

No matter how noble the cause, it is a cruel and unusual punishment, and a violation of one's rights as a human being to be given a truncated Gospel that is so close to truth and yet so far.

Liberation Theologians must realize that there is a vast difference between the redistribution of wealth and possessions, administered with political promises that likely will not be kept, and the distribution of the Body of Our Lord Jesus Christ, ministering the blood of His sacrifice, fulfilling promises that are still to have their ultimate realization and fulfillment.

One of the most striking indictments against Liberation Theology has been written by Henri Nouwen, a Catholic priest: "Jesus' first temptation was to be relevant: to turn stones into bread. Oh, how often have I wished I could do that! Walking through the 'young towns' on the outskirts of Lima, Peru, where children die from malnutrition and contaminated water, I would not have been able to reject the magical gift of making the dusty stone-covered streets into places where people could pick up any of the thousands of rocks and discover that they were croissants, coffee cakes, or fresh-baked buns, and where they could fill their cupped hands with stale water from the cisterns and joyfully realize that what they were drinking was delicious milk. Aren't we priests and ministers called to help people, to feed the hungry, and to save those who are starving? Are we not called to do something that makes people realize that we do make a difference in their lives? Aren't we called to heal the sick, feed the hungry, and alleviate the suffering of the poor? Jesus was faced with these same questions, but when he was asked to prove his power as the Son of God by the relevant behavior of changing stones into bread, he clung to his mission to proclaim the word and said, 'Human beings live not by bread alone, but by every word that comes from the mouth of God.'"

In the dimness of the candlelight, Rosa's three sisters sat facing her and Gustavo, the living relics of this fantastic dream. But it wasn't a dream. Wasn't Gustavo sick? Yes, but now he was alive! The power of the Healing God had brought Gustavo back from death, and given him the gift of life! It was true! Not more than three hours ago, they sat beneath the heat of the burning sun and waited for the wails of death to echo in their ears. Just a moment past in time, Pasquala uttered doubtful prayers and flinched before the will of Yajval Balamil, the only god she knew .

A rare breeze stole through the dark spaces in the slatted walls of the hut, fingering the candlelight and rustling the dried corn cobs that hung from the roof. Pasquala's memory conjured up images from the past and twirled them about in her mind. She heard the drunken footsteps of her father stumbling up the path, fist clenched around the neck of the posh bottle that sloshed in a hollow warning of his presence. She felt the blood trickling off her forehead, painting the evidence of his anger across her face. Then the heat of the candle's fire, burning a bridge to the spirit's realm, and igniting a panic in the chicken's breast. A cry, blood's thirsty smell, fire, fear. Onward it flung her to the blood pool spreading beneath her mother's fallen body, mosquitoes and sweat on her neck, the terror of the gunshots ringing in her ears, and again, the candles burning blindly down to darkness. She had fled from the coast and hidden in her new life back at the village in the mountains, yet the phantoms followed her trail. They followed into her sleep, cold breathing at her back and raking talons in her dreams, crying out their blood thirst.

But this Jehovah had no blood thirst. It was quenched already. The phantoms fled at his command, and fear ran from his presence.

"Yes."

Her tiny body cried the words before her mouth could contain them.

"Yes!"

She reached her arms towards the sky. With all the longing in her lonely heart, with every trembling fear that flings a child into her mother's arms, Pasquala leaped into Jehovah's grip.

"Yes!" It was a song her sisters joined, hand in hand and hearts in heaven's light they drank the sweet simplicity of belief. Again the tireless angels lifted wings in delirious songs of celebration. Maker God stooped low to touch the earth below and gathered His new children into His arms.

In an instant, Pasquala shed a twelve year sentence to a cage of fear and danced into the circle of heaven's shining warriors.

The phantoms fled. The spirits trembled. The demons hid. Fear fell. And the Maker God, Jehovah-Rafa, the One Who Heals, filled the heart of this Chiapan night.

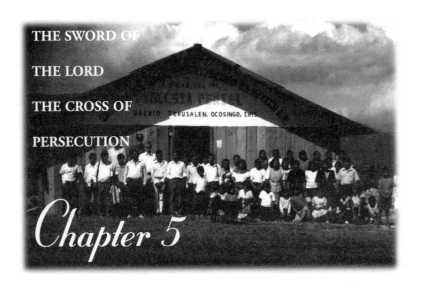

THE SWORD OF THE LORD THE CROSS OF PERSECUTION

Chapter 5

*. . .You have carefully followed my doctrine,
manner of life, purpose, faith, long-suffering,
love, perseverance, persecutions, afflictions
. . . and out of them all the Lord delivered me.
Yes, and all who desire to live godly in Christ Jesus
will suffer persecution. But evil men and impostors
will grow worse and worse, deceiving
and being deceived. But as for you, continue in the
things which you have learned and been assured of,
knowing from whom you have learned them,
and that from childhood you have known the
Holy Scriptures, which are able to make you wise
for salvation through faith which is in Christ Jesus.
All Scripture is given by inspiration of God,
and is profitable for doctrine, for reproof,
for correction, for instruction in righteousness,
that the man of God may be complete,
thoroughly equipped for every good work.*

2 Timothy 3:10-16

THE SWORD OF THE LORD

Second-generation missionary Bible translator Edward Aulie and his associate climbed up and down steep hills through thick jungle ravines for many hours. Finally the path widened. Ahead of them was the small village of Bebedeto. The villagers gave them food and drink and shelter for the night, so that they could continue their journey the next day.

As darkness fell, they lay down on a mat that had been graciously provided by the villagers. Aulie was about to close his eyes when he heard a voice quietly calling out his name. He sat up and answered. Lucio, one of the village leaders, stepped meekly into the dark room. Aulie lit a candle to indicate a welcome. Lucio, looking at the ground, slowly began to speak. He told of having lost two of his precious children to disease and now his one-week-old baby was vomiting and dying of the "disease." With pleading eyes, he looked into Aulie's face, begging him to help. Aulie knew the problem was dysentery, but had no medicine with him. Lucio hung his head in hopelessness. Aulie reached over and touched his shoulder, quietly explaining that there was other medicine. Lucio lifted his head, hopefully, as Aulie explained, "God is the Creator and has in His hands to give and to take away."

He explained to Lucio that God teaches us in His Word to "pray in faith according to His will, that we may find life." Lucio's wife was just outside the hut with the little baby. As Lucio beckoned, she carried him in and laid him in front of Aulie. The child was in the last stages of dysentery and would not live another day unless the Lord intervened. They all began to pray fervently for the restoration of the child. They read from the Bible and sang hymns of hope late into the night, until they felt they had done all they could do. Lucio's wife picked up the little infant, still vomiting, and silently left for home. Lucio followed her.

Aulie, back on his mat, tossed and turned between sleep and prayer until it was time to rise and continue their walk to the small village of Chulum. For two weeks Aulie and his associates worked there with the pastors of the church.

As they prepared to return home, Aulie was told that someone had come who was anxious to see him. Stepping quickly through the door was Lucio. Aulie did not know how to react. Had his baby died? Should he offer his condolences? Lucio excitedly recounted what had happened. "The baby got well right after you left, and today he is crying, laughing, and healthy."

Then Lucio turned very serious. Again he looked at the ground. "But now," he said, "my seven-year-old has the disease and has little life left."

Aulie, knowing that he would be returning to Lucio's village on his way home, had purchased some dysentery medicine to take to him. He reached in a bag and began to show Lucio how to administer it. Lucio interrupted him, "No, no, not that medicine. I came for prayer. I have hiked five hours. I could have gone to a closer village if I had wanted that kind of medicine. That medicine does not work as well. I want prayer like you gave my baby so my elder son will get well too."

Lucio's son recovered from dysentery. He, like his brother, experienced the promise of Psalm 107:20, "He sent His WORD and healed them and delivered them from their destruction." Missionary Aulie brought to them that which is ". . .of God, living and powerful, sharper than a two-edged sword, piercing of soul and spirit, and of joints and marrow, and is a discerner of thought and intents of the heart."

It was this "sword" that the early Catholic church did not want the people to read or study. Martin Luther was told by his superiors that it would create great confusion if all the people, especially the ordinary ones, were allowed to read the Bible and interpret it for themselves. Everyone would have their own theology. So, in many churches the Bible, if there was one, was chained to the pulpit so that no one could take it away to study it.

In a nation that was nearly 100 percent Catholic, even the priests had only limited access to a Bible. Even then, it was written in Latin, a language they could not readily understand.

That all began to change in the early part of the nineteenth century. Historian Kenneth Scott LaTourette reports that an agent of the American Bible Society was permitted into Mexico as early as 1820. In Mexico's war with the United States, soldiers of the U.S. army distributed portions of the Bible to Mexican soldiers. It was the first time they had seen the "black Bible", a name given because most Bibles from the U.S. at that time were bound in black. LaTourette also traces the entry of a few Bibles into Mexico back to Melinda Rankin, who started a Bible School in the border town of Brownsville, Texas before 1861.

Ironically, politics played a major role in making the Bible generally available in Spanish as well as in indigenous languages. In 1936, President Cardenas, no friend of Christianity, felt that the entry of Protestants and the Bible into Mexico might weaken the Catholic Church's hold on the Indians and all of Mexico. With that in mind, he invited Wycliffe Bible Translators to come into Mexico, and in 1936 they began translating the Bible into many Indian languages. Even the non-political minded would later admit that these translations of the indigenous languages made an important linguistic contribution to the entire nation.

This breakthrough was not without its price, however. A sword, properly wielded, is certain to divide, which is not a painless procedure. The Word, which intrinsically carries the power to divide truth and error, at times divided villages and families. In 1981, Catholic leaders, assisted by the Marxists, charged the Wycliffe translators with "ethnocide and cultural expropriation," and convinced the government to revoke the forty-year old agreement with Wycliffe, ordering their eviction from the country. However, they were about to find out, as had Lucio, that "God is the Creator and He has in His hands to give and to take away." Today, Wycliffe continues to translate the Word of God for the people of Mexico.

In the eyes of many, the "Black Book" was associated with those who "protested" certain teachings of the traditional Catholic Church. In Mexico today, a high regard for the authority and power found in the "Black Book" has come to be associated with the term evangelical. According to Dr. Henry Aulie, the beginning of the evangelical movement in Chiapas is tied directly to the Bible's availability and translation into the language of the common man.

From 1907 to 1914, an American with unknown affiliations by the name of Sutherland traveled as an evangelist to various villages in Tabasco, Chiapas and Guatemala. Between 1911 and 1912 he traveled from ranch to ranch, distributing gospel literature. At a coffee plantation in Tumbala, Chiapas, owned by a man of Catholic persuasion known only as Morison, Sutherland was warned not to evangelize his workers. After spending a night with Morison, he went to the village of Tumbala and met a mestizo by the name of Eplidio Asutdillo. While keeping his pledge to Morison not to "evangelize," he left Christian literature with Elpidio.

Elpidio's son Gonzalo, a foreman on Morison's ranch, read the literature and was impressed enough to order more from the addresses printed on the tracts.

Elpido was a heavy drinker who worshiped a statue of a Black Christ and would travel five hours on foot by trail to worship this statue in Tila. The priest in Tila protested to Elpidio that his son Gonzalo was coming to the village and distributing forbidden Protestant literature. Elpidio confronted his son. Gonzalo asked his father to read the literature and then to burn up whatever he felt was not true. Leaving the book and tracts and matches with his father, Gonzalo went back to work. Upon his return he found the literature intact, His father had been persuaded that the priests were mistaken in their teachings. One of the books was the prohibited "Black Book."

Elpidio believed what he read in the "Black Book" and was converted. He stopped drinking, and some members of his family did the same. A mestiza plantation owner made a profession of faith in Jesus Christ and opened her home to Bible teaching and preaching. A number of mestizos were converted in those early years. Unfortunately, many "conversions" were more a reaction and statement against Roman Catholicism than a deep conversion to Christ. In spite of that, the evangelical church was planted and continued to grow.

A Presbyterian pastor from Las Casas visited the new believers. A man of vision, he believed that evangelizing should be a natural outworking of discipleship. He appointed twelve of the Chol men to go out to evangelize.

One of the twelve later gave his story.

"I made my first evangelistic trip at the age of thirteen. We went to the village of Istelja. Nobody believed there. Later that year we went with Chol believers to the Providencia, where Abram Astudillos lived. Abram believed. I carried a projector to a ranch owned by Abram's brother and he and his family received us with friendliness and listened to the gospel. The Indians were open in all the villages we visited.

The people in many of the villages continued drinking . There was a lot of killing. It took seven to eight years to cut lose from their terrible past. But they finally did.

Once we went into a village and nobody would take us in, so we slept in a pig house. First the new believers stopped drinking. They they stopped gong to the fiestas. Later they threw away their idols and pictures of saints. They went to the authorities to legalize their marriages. They also stopped calling the shamans, (witch doctors) to heal the sick and to pray to the shamans that their corn would grow. They put their trust in Jesus Christ."

These early believers did not fear those who were opposed to the gospel. Through the Word of God they knew they had found salvation, and they spread the message about Jesus Christ wherever they went. There was great openness to the gospel in many villages.

The gospel story has been repeated thousands of times since then, and is still being told today. But again, it is not without a price. To bring to a people the "Sword of the Word of the Lord" requires that we also are willing to bear the Author's Cross.

God greatly used two young women to take the Word of Jesus from Philadelphia to Mexico. Evelyn Woodward and Mariana Slocum were friends at Wilson College in Chambersberg, Pennsylvania. While there, neither imagined that they would later find themselves translating God's Word into a foreign language, the true "heart language" of the people of Chiapas. At a Wycliffe camp in 1940, the Lord reunited the two friends and created a ministry partnership with one common purpose and burden, to bring the Good News to Mexico. They weren't sure how, but they were committed to following the Lord, trusting that He would direct their paths, even through the jungles of Chiapas.

Hearing from conference speakers about the Chols in the southeastern part of the country, Evelyn prayed, "Lord, send missionaries to the Chols." Mariana prayed, "Lord, send us!" By September of that year, God had answered both prayers. The girls were accepted by the Townsend Group (not yet named Wycliffe Bible Translators) to work in Mexico. From Mexico city they traveled two days and nights by train to Arriaga, four hours by bus to Tuxtla, four hours by mail-truck and ten by mule to Las Camas, followed days later by a half-hour ride in a small plane to Yajalon and finally weeks later, six hours by mule to reach Chola.

They were received at the Alianza, the Morisons' coffee plantation at Tumbala where Sutherland and another preacher named Granados had been received more than twenty years earlier. This was another step in carrying out God's purpose for the Chols. The seed which had been planted by Sutherland and Granados was now to be watered. Marianna went on to the Tamial field the next year, while Evelyn remained with the Morisons. Mr. Morison, a Yale graduate and a Catholic, had married a Tumbala girl and settled at the Alianza. One by one over the years, all of that family came to know Christ, and one of them, Mary, became a Wycliffe translator in Ecuador. Through their hospitality, the Morisons were used by God to advance the gospel in Chol country.

During those two years, Evelyn and her new co-worker, Ruth Hitchner, lived with the Morisons at Alianza and studied Chol, for no village would receive them. Finally, they were accepted by the village of Hidalgo. Evelyn and Ruth were given a hut by a young Indian, who had built it for himself and his new wife, but believing it to be haunted, had abandoned it.

Evelyn and her co-worker found that the house was too small for efficient work, so they asked for permission to enlarge it. The matter was discussed by the Indians. Some said, "They have good hearts. Let them build another room. What have we to fear from two women?" Others replied, "No, they are giving us honey now but when they have their own land in our village they will turn against us, or others will come in their place and will oppose us."

This disagreement led to an official document, with a thumb print signature, warning them against building the addition to the house in Hidalgo. This decision was reversed when Evelyn, ignoring the document drafted by the school teacher, appealed to the town fathers, and received authority to expand the home.

At the time the women began their work in Chiapas, men always traveled armed. But while Indians traveled with companions and carried machetes, Evelyn traveled fearlessly. Stephen E. Slocum tells of a journey Evelyn made to visit her friend, Marianna, after she had transferred to the Tzeltal tribe: "The story of Evelyn's ride will furnish a glimpse of their courage and stamina. Other rides, famous in song and story, pale in comparison. Paul Revere was less than two hours in the saddle and was picked up by British patrols before he reached Concord. Sheridan's ride was an afternoon gallop over a main highway. But Evy's ride was a twenty-five hour epic of rain, mud and blackness over an unknown trail through Indian country."

Evelyn's destination was the outpost where Marianna Slocum, her companion during the first year among the Chols, lived among the Tzetals. Securing a horse in the jumping-off town of Las Casas and the owner of the horse as a guide over the unfamiliar trail, Evelyn went out on what should have been a one day trip. However, the guide intended to double his pay by making it a two day trip. Late that day, when they should have been nearing Marianna's house, Evelyn came to the Indian village of Tenejapa, which was only half way to her destination.

The guide planned to stop in Tenejapa, but because it was a wild place filled with drunken Indians, Evelyn insisted on going on, sure that they must soon reach their destination. A dark night overtook them with a tropical downpour. It was too dark to see anything, even the horse beneath her, much less the trail. Then, quite suddenly, a woman appeared out of the darkness carrying a torch. Evelyn asked her for shelter, but the woman dropped her torch and fled into the darkness, apparently frightened by the white girl.

The animal followed the trail in the darkness until it turned aside into a field and stopped. The guide gave up attempting to push the animal on, wrapped himself in his serape and lay down in the mud to sleep. At an altitude of 7,000 feet and drenched to the skin, Evelyn shivered in the cold. All that night she remained in the saddle, getting some warmth from the body of the horse. When daylight came she roused her guide and continued on. The trail led down a steep mountainside, so winding and narrow that it was even dangerous by day. Evelyn could only marvel at the Lord's protection in causing the animal to turn aside to the cornfield that night.

When she finally reached Marianna's house later that morning, there she was, coming out into the yard, completely surprised to see her. In sudden remembrance, Marianna exclaimed, "Why Evy, happy birthday!"

Upheld in spirit through the long sleepless night by the very real sense of the Lord's presence, Evelyn had recalled verse after verse of the Scriptures which brought comfort and hope. "This poor man cried unto the Lord, and the Lord heard him and delivered him from all his distresses." But now that the ordeal was behind her, she wept in relief.

The coming of the girls to Tumbala converged under God's hand with His work of grace among the Indians to turn them to Himself. On May 6, 1941, Evelyn wrote to friends:

". . .One day twenty-some Chol believers filed into our yard, having set out at day-break and walked many miles over tortuous mountain trails to worship with us that morning. They were led by don Chanti, a mestizo who had become a Christian through reading the Scriptures, and who then, with no formal preparation, but with the love of God shed abroad in his heart, had set out to make Christ known to the Chols. Traveling from one village to another and to scattered huts he has reached many with the gospel; and wherever he goes, it seems, the Spirit of God touches hearts. Now there are several different congregations of Christians in this region.

. . .Later, on four successive Sundays we ourselves, speaking through an interpreter, had services for the 50 to 60 Indians who met with us weekly in Tumbala in the absence of don Chanti. How great the contrast between this group and another group of Indians which we saw previously in Tumbala. There, in a room dimly lighted by candles, knelt several dozen Chols, drunkenly chanting prayers to a plaster image of San Miguel. Some were so intoxicated that they lay sprawled out on the floor; while one with feverish anxiety and intensity besought the help of a god who could not hear nor answer. Here was no joy, no peace, no assurance; here only superstition, sin, and despair."

As soon as the women knew enough of the language, they prepared records of hymns and messages, which were then produced by Gospel Recordings. The first run of records made available in 1943 was greatly used by God in the spread of the gospel. The Indians listened to the records over and over again, and in so doing learned the hymns and the elements of the gospel message at the same time.[1]

Henry Aulie came to the Chol field in 1946, beginning a lifetime of rewarding work, work to which he actually came reluctantly. Hearing the call of God to missionary service as a Junior at Wheaton College, he stubbornly put it aside to continue what he had begun to do, to prepare for business. After college, God patiently allowed five exciting years in government and public accounting. Then He graciously opened his eyes to see that he had been pursuing his own way rather than God's. In the summer of 1946 he found both his life work and his life partner, Evelyn Woodward. After further training at Camp Wycliffe, he joined the organization. He married Evelyn upon his arrival in Mexico that September. Later that fall he had his introduction to the village of Hidalgo and to the Chol country.

As the Wycliffe Missionaries finished their translation work, the Indians of Chiapas at last had the Bible in their own language, but it still needed to be distributed and preached and taught. This would be, and still is, the job of the national preachers and lay evangelists.

One of those preachers, Christobal Arcos, tells his story.

"I went to Allenda. As I was walking along I saw a man hiding himself behind a tree. He had a gun. He was looking at me. He fired the gun. The shot passed near but did not hit me. I went to speak to the man. 'What are you shooting at? Why do you want to shoot me?' He replied, 'I am shooting birds.' I told him, 'It's not birds you're shooting at. You want to shoot me. I want to tell you that you should not do evil. If you had shot me you would not gain anything. If you do evil you will go to the place where you will pay for your sin. That's why I came to your village, to tell all the men that they should not do evil, killing and stealing. I came to tell you about the Living God.' I reached Allende with that man who accompanied me. I went to his house. At dusk Miguel Vasquez loaned me his house to stay there overnight.

There was a sick boy who was losing blood through his mouth and nose. I prayed for him. The next day the boy got well. So I was taken to other houses to pray because there were many who were sick, and they saw the boy who got well. I was about 20 years of age when I began to work in Allende. They asked me, 'Who is teaching you? Where did you get your book?' After about six months the man who tried to shoot me believed on Christ. The other sick for whom we prayed got well gradually. They did not get well right away. Those who were in the house of the boy who was healed on the following day believed on Christ at that time. Only once after that did Miguel drink liquor. After a little while he threw away the picture which he had been worshipping. Miguel was the first believer. All but a few of the families in the village believed.

Cuctiepa was a village of scattered houses at the edge of La Cueva where there are ruins of our ancestors. When we went to La Cueva, the people of Cuctiepa came to La Cueva to ask, 'What stories are you believing?' The La Cueva people replied, 'We are being taught the Word of God. The things that you are doing are not right. The God we believe in is teaching us.' The Cuctiepa people said, 'We want to hear this, too. When your visitors come to preach, send someone to tell us so that we may come to hear.' So we went to Cuctiepa. We told them that we have a new teacher, our Lord above. They asked us, 'Where is He now?' I answered, 'He is in heaven, but He is also here with us.' They asked again, 'What are we required to do?' We told them, 'You are to obey the commands of God. You are not to do wickedness. You are not to drink liquor, nor to consult witch doctors. Turn from evil. Christ came to seek us. He came to buy us with His blood. If we believe, we will be saved. He changes our hearts.' Only three men believed. When we returned a half year later four more believed."

Dr. Aulie summarizes the work of both translators and the indigenous lay pastors: "The nationals have experienced deliverance from their fears and from a miserable existence. They could not keep it hidden. They shared the message with their fellows. The gospel took root in their hearts and early began to bear fruit in their outreach to the villages. They had a growing knowledge of the Scriptures, which they were receiving piecemeal in their own language, even in mimeographed editions. They had an increasing grasp of the grace that there is in Jesus Christ and a growing love for Him. They worked with faith in Him with excitement as they saw the Word of God prosper amongst their own people."

They were not alone. As the Indians carried on the task of evangelism and teaching in the villages, the missionaries learned the languages and worked on translations while living with the people. The missionaries ministered medically, and taught the Indians how to read their own language. They continued translating the scripture, training lay people to do their own translating. The missionaries wrote and translated hymns, and taught a number of young people to play musical instruments. An evangelical church thus emerged, and began to flourish as a "partnership in mission" between the Indians and the missionaries.

The draw of God's Word can be seen in the following 1997 letter written by missionary translators, Ken and Elaine Jacobs.

"Around ten o'clock one Sunday morning, Elaine and I happened to walk past the door of 'Caridad,' a Mexican Catholic church in the barrio of Santo Domingo in San Cristobal, Chiapas, Mexico. The large old church overflowed with Chamula Indians, hundreds of them, they were spilling out the large wooden doors onto the street. The overflow crowd of Chamulas on the outside pushed on tip-toes trying to see and hear what was going on inside.

The heathen Chamula witch doctors will often bring a sick tribesman all the way from their tribal area into the Mexican town of San Cristobal to perform their heathen healing ceremony near the colorful altar in one of the many Mexican Catholic churches. I assumed this must be an important heathen Chamula to command such a large crowd of followers.

I squeezed by the Chamula onlookers outside. Pushing my way through the crowded entrance, my height advantage rewarded me with a clear vision over these shorter Mayan Chamula Indians standing behind the last rows of benches in the church. What I saw and heard was not what I thought was gong on. I spoke as loudly and urgently as I dared to Elaine, still standing outside the door, 'You have to come in to see and hear this.'

This was far more than a healing ceremony. Here sat a large congregation of Chamula Indians respectfully listening to the Scripture. This was much more than a mere physical healing ceremony. This was the cleansing washing of pure water - the washing of the Word of God. And not the Word of God in the Spanish language the Chamulas do no really understand. This was the language of the heart and soul - their own Mayan Chamula tongue. The Chamula leader was sharing from the translated Chamula New Testament - the New Testament that Elaine and I had spend many difficult years preparing for them. He was speaking to them from the book of Hebrews: 'Jesus took his own blood and went into the very presence of God - the Holy of Holies. My Brethren, just think, because of Jesus we are free from our sins. Now we know we are accepted by God.'

The following Sunday, Elaine and I returned early. We looked forward to the opportunity to meet and to visit with these animated Chamula leaders. We commended them for their love and respect for the Word of God, as well as their joy in sharing God's truth with hundreds of their spiritually hungry tribespeople. They knew that the whole Bible was being translated into their language and were delighted to hear from us that the day of its publication was getting closer every day. So many faithful people have had a part in getting the whole Bible into the hands of the Chamula world."

But know this, that in the last days perilous times will
come: For men will be lovers of themselves, lovers of money, boast-
ers, proud, blasphemers, disobedient to parents, unthankful, unholy,
unloving, unforgiving, slanderers, without self-control, brutal,
despisers of good, traitors, headstrong, haughty,
lovers of pleasure rather than lovers of God,
having a form of godliness but denying its power.
And from such people turn away!

2 Timothy 3:1-5

THE CROSS OF PERSECUTION

The shadow of the cross on top of the white washed facade began to spread across the square, in the village of Amentage De Valle, in the Teopisca Municipality of Chiapas. Siesta time was nearly over, but not everyone had rested.

The morning message by the padre alerted the people that it was time to take care of "a very serious problem, one that affected all of them." The caciques looked at each other knowingly. There were those who looked forward to the anticipated action and trouble, but others simply stared at the floor. More subdued than usual, people gathered their families and headed home after the service as the caciques and church leadership huddled together in a circle talking, gesturing, and finally joining their families as they walked down the paved street to their own homes, which were conspicuously set apart by the electrical lines connecting them to the church. Inside their spacious homes, with wooden floors and glass windows, they reclined on comfortable chairs, waiting for the soup, beans, tortillas and fruit, and the beer to wash it all down. When they stopped eating, it was not because the food ran out, but because they were too full to do anything but take a "siesta" on their store-bought mattresses, as ceiling fans refreshed them with cool air. It was a lifestyle they did not want to lose, and today they would do what had to be done to make sure that they didn't.

The other, more common families, walked down dusty, unpaved streets to their waddle and straw houses. The only breeze they felt came from glassless window openings. They sat on the floor eating a simple meal of tortillas and black beans. Because it was Sunday, there might even be a piece of chicken. None ate until they were full, but until the food was gone. They then lay back on the dirt floor for their siesta. It was a standard of living they would have gladly exchanged for something better, but the gods had not been happy with them this year, and the crops had been bad. The times were, as they had been all of their lives, difficult. But they would get better, it was hoped, because they had burned candles to the saints twice this week, to make sure that the "saints and sinners" saw them as they put their few sweaty pesos and centavos into the offering box. They had trouble napping. They knew what the padre meant when he said they had to "take care of a serious problem," and though they didn't want to, they would have to participate. They could not afford to have the caciques angry with them. After all, they still owed money for the eleven festivals of each of the last two years, and though their house was little more than shelter, it was all they had. It too, was owned by the caciques.

In several homes no one slept. Even the children sensed that this afternoon would be a time of great trouble. For nearly a year, some of the village families had publicly stated that they no longer believed the saints had power, and that they would no longer pay homage to them. A foreigner in another village had given them a holy book in their own language, which told of the one true God whose name is Jesus Christ. This God wanted everyone to follow Him. That would mean they would no longer participate in the many festivals honoring the deities. They would no longer get drunk on posh, or buy candles for the saints, or firecrackers to shoot into the air to awaken the gods. They also would not give extra money offerings to the church.

The problem was not a lack of belief in the saints and the many gods. The problem was simply economic in nature. Evangelicals no longer bought posh or candles, no longer gave offerings, or bought extra fiesta foods, or bought costumes for the parades. These were the "necessities" of everyday Catholic life in the village, and were available for sale only through the cacique's local monopoly.

At first, a family might try saying they had no money, because the gods had looked down on them with disfavor. The caciques then insisted they loan the needed money at a 125 percent interest rate. Two festivals were enough to put many people in debt to the cacique for the rest of their lives, and through them, to the church.

A small wisp of hope came to the small hut, as the hot afternoon sunlight began to recede. "Maybe they'll do nothing today," said one, "maybe this time it will be different."

Suddenly, cutting into the minds of those sleeping and those anxiously awake, a voice from the loudspeakers mounted on the top of the church blared across the village. With the sound, all hope was removed that today might be different.

"All the people of the village are to gather in the square at once for a special meeting! I repeat, all the people of the village are to gather in the square for a special meeting!"

Everyone knew what it meant; a few families had touched the seat of power, and they must be dealt with.

As people began to slowly make their way to the city square, those who remained in their homes knew that what they were going to experience was not unique to Chiapas. It was something that happened to "evangelicals." They knew, as did the the parents of the little girl who died of burns in the village of Zactsu, and the two little boys who were killed with machetes after a meeting to solve "the problem that had to be taken care of." The persecution of evangelicals was rarely reported in the national press, and even more rarely was there any retribution for elected officials whose political election had been strongly "recommended to the villagers" by the local caciques and priests.

Newspaper headlines, if the stories had been printed, would have been a litany of abuse disgracing not only Chiapas and its leadership, but all of Mexico as well. Even the most skeptical observers, who support the self-called Human Rights organizations that believe that the religious persecution of evangelicals is not necessarily a Human Rights violation, would cringe to read the following:

Jan. 21, 1966:
Three evangelicals are shot at in the village of Yaalvacash; a little girl is wounded in the face.

1972
Twenty-two indigenous evangelicals are murdered in Nayarit.

Aug. 15, 1976
600 evangelicals are expelled from various villages in San Juan Chamula.

Aug. 22, 1976
Twenty-six families are beaten, jailed and expelled from the village of Joltzemen.

Jul. 24, 1981
Brother Miguel "Cashlan" Gomez Hernandez, the first evangelical preacher in Chamula, is savagely murdered; they ripped off his nose, an ear, his lips, and his scalp, gouged out his eyes and hung him.

Apr. 2, 1993
Vicente Mendez Velazquez is murdered by cacique expellers in Mitontic, Chiapas. His burned corpse was found one month after he had disappeared.

Jan. 17, 1994
A mob, armed with pick-axes and spades, destroyed the church that was being built in the village of Panales, Ixmiquilpan, Hidalgo state.

Jan. 25, 1994
Ten families were expelled in San Andres Zabache because they refused to contribute money for catholic celebrations.

Sep. 29, 1994
A group of approximately 300 caciques murdered the family members Migues Mendez Santiz, Miguel Lopez Perez, and Veronica Diez Jimenez, in Icalumtic, San Juan Chamula, Chiapas. They also raped Octavia Mendez Diez, fourteen years old. Four caciques killed her parents in front of her. Thirteen children became orphans and a widow was shot.

Aug. 24, 1995
Domingo Lopez Rangel informed that more than 35,000 natives (Tzetzales and Totziles) have been expelled in the area of Los Altos, Chiapas, during the last 20 years "because they have left the catholic faith and professed the evangelical faith." They were forced to leave more than 247,000 acres of land.

Though the headlines would make sordid reading, the detailed report is more gruesome as seen by this story from Mexico City:

MEXICO CITY (NNI - June ll, 1991) More than 300 Christians are now living as refugees in the compound of a church in the southern Mexico state capital of Oaxaca, after a violent mid-April assault by townspeople hostile to the presence of evangelical Protestants in their village.

On May 15, three leaders of the Maranatha church of San Miguel Aloapan, district of Ixtlan de Juarez, filed a complaint with the official National Commission for Human Rights in Mexico City, after surviving a brutal attack by townspeople who forced them to flee. They also appealed to evangelical leaders for help and said they were willing to bring the entire group to Mexico City if necessary to find a just resolution to their case.

According to Adan Jimenez Ruiz, president of the Fraternity of Evangelical Christian Pastors of Oaxaca (COPACEO) and pastor of the San Miguel Aloapan Maranatha Church, members of his church were invited to attend a government-sponsored congress in the state capital on April 19. Transportation was provided for the journey, but no sooner had their trip gotten under way when townspeople blocked the highway and launched an attack on the buses.

According to eyewitnesses, men women and children were forcibly dragged off the buses, including one pregnant woman; a two-month old baby was "savagely" beaten; and at least 10 men were stripped of their clothes and robbed.

Jimenez said the men were "publicly exposed during daylight to children who at that moment were coming out of school. Many of the men were dragged [about] and badly beaten. Others were tortured and imprisoned."

Those detained were released the following day and reportedly fled San Miguel Aloapan with their families.

Protestants first came to San Miguel Aloapan about five years ago and ever since, say believers, they have been persecuted for their faith. Just two days prior to the attack, Baldomero Cruz Alavez, a member of the Maranatha church, was reportedly beaten, imprisoned, tortured and briefly hanged by the local police. He survived and was released two days later.

On this dusty, hot Sunday afternoon, it is the turn of the people of Amatenange del Valle. The meeting was over in the city square; the decision had been made. The Evangelicals must go.

Seventeen Presbyterian families were attacked in their homes by their former neighbors, lead by caciques carrying cudgels, axes, and machetes. Men, women and children heard the attackers coming, and fled into the forest without food or protection from the elements. Their homes were ransacked. Their personal belongs were thrown into the street and their houses set ablaze. Hiding in the forest, these evangelicals were still close enough to smell the smoke from their burning homes. They realized that all they would have to start a new future would be the items they carried with them. They could hear the shouting from the loudspeakers atop the church: "We have chased all the evangelicals out of our village; no one is to have anything to do with them!" followed by muffled cheers.

It had all begun in one man's home. Though in his early thirties he felt very old, and certain that he was dying. His wife also became very ill. "If we both die," he thought, "who will take care of our children?" He sent for the shaman, or local witch doctor. The shaman performed a few rituals on the wife, as the husband drank his numbing posh. The shaman then took out his knife and cut an incision in her arm. As the blood flowed onto the ground, he scooped some of it up in a little container. He said he could read the blood, that it would tell him what was wrong, and whether anyone was to blame for her sickness, so that appropriate action could be taken.

The wife's health deteriorated. Fever caused her to become irrational. The husband and four children gathered around her to watch her die. The children cried, the husband cursed the gods and drank his posh.

Then one of the children said he knew of a family in their village that worshiped a God who could heal their mommy. Desperate, the father sent the child to fetch these "troublemakers" whom he had heard about but vowed never to allow into his home. Now he was desperate.

When the evangelical couple entered, he moved away to a corner. They knelt beside his dying wife. Though the husband could not hear all they were saying, he heard the words "Dios, Dios, and Jesu Cristo" repeated. As the woman stayed with his sick wife, the man took the husband aside to talk to him. He told him that the Lord Jesus Christ heals in various ways. They prayed that the wife would get well, but they also wanted to give her some medicine they had purchased in San Cristobal. He then explained that the Lord uses medicine from man, as well as man's prayers, to heal people.

The husband wasn't drunk enough to forget that if the Shaman found out about the evangelicals in his home, he would cast demons into the house and they would all die - father, mother and children. He argued for some time with the man, but finally relented. The man and woman gave his wife medicine, prayed awhile longer, and then left, saying they would be back in a couple of hours. The husband sat and stared at his wife. After a few moments, she looked over at him and spoke her first words in three days. "I feel better," she mumbled, "I think their god is more powerful than ours." Frightened, the husband moved beside her. She smiled and went to sleep.

Two days later, the shaman came back with a bottle of posh and his paraphernalia, asking if she had died yet. When told that she was not only alive, but had cooked supper for the family the night before, the shaman began to take the credit for reading the blood correctly. The husband, shaking with fear, knew what he had to do. He explained exactly what had happened to the Shaman. When the Shaman left he knew it would only be minutes before there would be a visit from some of the cacique's "bully boys." Back in the house, he saw the smile on his wife's face. He knew that her new God was more powerful than his. Maybe her God could heal him, too. Three days later, the man and woman who had previously been shunned from the house now kneeled in prayer beside him. It was the only medicine he needed.

The husband, wife, and children joined several other evangelical families in Sunday worship. All refused to participate in the

Catholic festivals any longer. In fact, the number of evangelicals had grown to fifteen families, and they wanted to build their own church, as no house was large enough to hold them. This was the "problem that needed to be solved." These were the troublemakers that the priest had denounced from the pulpit, while the caciques nodded in agreement.

While some in the village celebrated the cleansing of the village with posh and bravado, the Evangelicals gathered in the forest and thanked Jesus Christ that they were worthy to suffer for Him. In the forest, they praised the Lord for fulfilling the promise in His word, that He would not give them any cross which was too heavy to bear.

Carla and Vernon Sterk have spent much of their adult life living with the Indians in Chiapas. Dr. Sterk's thesis, The Dynamics Of Persecution, explains the dominant role persecution has played in building and strengthening the body of our Lord in that country. Sterk points out that there was intense persecution in the days of Cortes, five centuries ago. Persecution of the evangelicals was rather sporadic in the 1930's, increased during the 1950's, and is becoming even more violent in the late 1990's.

The cause of persecution has always been the same: anything which threatens the power base of existing authority is attacked-sometimes unmercifully.

The present cycle of persecution began in the late 1950's when "Four Presbyterian Chols from the village of Tumbala were jailed for almost five years in Tuxtla Gutierres, the capital of Chiapas, due to the false accusation of having burned the Roman Catholic Church in Tumbala." Then "several itinerant evangelists were jailed "for preaching a Gospel that was different than that preached by the predominate religious body."

Those in authority soon realized that the Gospel acts like a prairie fire. If you stomp on it to put it out, the sparks could fly in every direction, igniting more fires. Consequently, they held the persecution of Evangelicals in check, but the gospel still spread rapidly. Besides the fear of flying sparks, the lack of organized persecution was attributed to the fact that the Chol tribe had no strong central organization which was threatened by this growth. That would later change. One consistent factor remains today: "When the Roman Catholic Church failed to promote persecution in the area, in that the villages were scattered about, they could not sustain the persecution against the evangelicals, opposition faded, and the body of believers grew to 30,000 by 1990," and is still growing today, to as many as 50,000.

One element is constant in persecution: violence. Sterk writes, "In 1956, the first congregation of Presbyterians in the municipality of Bachajon was attacked during worship service by a group of twenty-five armed assassins who were backed by the local Roman Catholic priest, Eleazar Mandujano. These assassins planned to kill the well-known leader of the Protestant evangelicals, but when the armed group found the Presbyterians singing hymns in his home, they opened fire on the entire group. When one of the evangelicals went outside to see what was happening he was killed instantly by the blasts from double-barreled shotguns. Two women in the house were wounded by gunfire, but were able to escape to the mountains from where they all watched the assassins burn the house in which they had been worshipping."

The persecution continued, and always for the same reasons. People were being converted to Christ. "1963," reports Sterk, "marked the first conversion of the first two Protestant evangelicals in the Chamula tribe." The body began to grow, and in 1964 they had their first house church service. The Gospel then began spreading to outlying districts, and with it came the inevitable persecution. "One of the chosen weapons was to burn evangelicals' houses at night. Sometimes those sleeping in the houses were burned to death. . . . Burning houses at night spread to almost all of the villages containing evangelicals. They spent most nights hiding in caves and mountains for the better part of a year."

The sparks of the Gospel continued to fly, as the priests and the caciques attempted to put out the fire. "By 1966," Sterk says, "the gospel had spread to several of the villages, in spite of the house burnings and killings. The tribal leaders attempted to stamp out the new belief of the Protestant evangelicals by assigning them jobs as traditional cargoes positions, a religious charge in the animistic folk religion. Most evangelicals refused to participate in the animistic services. As the persecution continued the body of believers continued to grow."

The evangelicals were then publicly warned to stop evangelizing, but they kept on, worshipping, witnessing and growing. More houses were burned in surrounding villages. It was at this time that the caciques realized they were losing control, that fewer and fewer people were attending mass, buying candles, images, and posh, or attending the festivals.

"The cleansing of many of the temples was, "as Sterk reports, "a serious threat to the caciques' power and authority." As a last attempt to stop the revival they issued a formal decree for the expulsion of all Protestant evangelicals, declaring they would "no longer respect the legal documents explaining the rights of Protestant evangelicals." All evangelicals were formally expelled and the death sentence was pronounced on any who dared to remain behind. Thirty thousand of these "religious refugees" now live on the outskirts of San Cristobal.

Another target for persecution is the missionary. A practice that began as early as 1949, and continues today, is reported by Sterk: "Shortly after the appearance of the first Protestant evangelicals in the Tseltal area, the tribal authorities presented formal accusations against the evangelicals in the Txeltal area, and two women missionaries, Marianna Slocum and Florence Gerde (mentioned earlier in this book). The formal accusation read:

"These women, as well as the other followers of that 'Protestant doctrine,' were preparing to burn the temple saints located in Oxchuc Catholic Church; these women are in reality men in disguise. They wear rubber breasts to make themselves look like women. As men, which they really are, they are sexually abusing the best young Txeltal girls. They eat dead people, bodies of persons that they have kidnapped, and then boil them alive in large pots in order to eat them."

When the absurdity of the charges was taken to the government, they were given no credence, but to satisfy the local officials, the government told the evangelicals they could remain only as long as they did not obligate anyone to become an evangelical.

One Human Rights group reports that the persecution in Chamula is not unique, and still continues today in municipalities like Amatenange del Valle, El Puerto, Las Margaritas, Zinacantan, and San Miguel Mitontia. Many families of believers in these cities have been forced to flee from their homes. The government's response to these abuses of human rights, which violate a number of Mexico's laws on individual constitutional rights, has been very sluggish. The evangelical Indians are often left homeless and forced to fend for themselves.

Open Doors, an organization that works with the persecuted church around the world reports, "These expulsions are usually violent, and in many cases, fatal. Innocent believers have been stabbed, stoned, and clubbed to death; women, including young girls, have been raped, in many cases by several men at a time, homes have been ransacked and burned, belongings and livestock stolen."

Their sins? Possessing, or even reading a Bible, listening to or singing Christian music, embracing Evangelical Christianity as their religion, meeting with other believers, even in their own homes for worship, building evangelical churches, no longer buying or drinking posh, and no longer participating in festivals laced with syncretism, which demand offerings of candles, flowers, animals, posh and other products sold by the caciques.

Many of the expelled believers have regrouped and founded new communities, little villages in the countryside, where all the residents are believers. The influence of the Christian culture is obvious in the names these refugees have chosen for both the towns and the streets: Nueva Vida (New Life), Betania (Bethany), Nueva Esperanza (New Hope), Palestina (Palestine), and most appropriately, Getsemani (Gethsemane).

Visitors to these new villages describe the orderly life, the picturesque little churches and the tranquillity that fill the life of the inhabitants, who are experiencing the reality of the presence of Christ in their midst. However, the phantom of violence is never completely absent. Residents must deal with continuous threats of attack by angry caciques and their co-conspirators.

Despite the violence, God has worked in some mysterious ways to defend His people in Chiapas. Easily verifiable are such testimonies as these:

"The caciques and their hoodlums came into our church and threw gasoline on the floor to burn it. When they tried to light it, it would not burn. We later asked one of them, 'Why did you come into our church and throw water all over the floor?'"

"The caciques led an attack against the refugee village of Mount of Olives when it was first being established, after its residents had been chased out of their homes. Some of the attackers with guns went around to the back of the village to ambush the residents, as others with clubs came at the village from the front. There was an intense battle, with both clubs and bullets flying over and onto the heads of the people. After the battle there was only one fatality. Lying about forty feet in front of the village was one man who had been shot - by his own men. When the caciques turned him over they saw it was the village witch doctor. They left him there for several hours until family members came to pick him up."

"Yesterday I was in the market and one of the men who helped to burn my house and chase me out of the village told me that he was a truck driver and he passed me every day on the road as I rode my bicycle. He said, 'I was going to run over you each time I saw you but I could not because you are surrounded by all those men.' I've always traveled alone."

"One day some of the villagers with clubs and guns were coming to our village. We met them before they got there so that they would not hurt our families, our women and children. We met at a small stream, inches deep and only a few feet wide. As the villagers arrived, they looked at us, and turned and ran back to their cacique leader to tell him that they could not swim across the river that separated them, the water was rushing too much and they would drown."

There are several observations to be made about persecution in Chiapas:

1. Evangelicals in Chiapas are, and have for many years been, victims of serious and measurable persecution. Though it may be true that in countries like China and India the number being persecuted is greater, that fact is of little comfort to a girl being raped, or a family weeping over a murdered father, a mother standing beside a house with all her personal belongings lying in a heap of ashes, or a family forced to hide in the forest.

2. The primary perpetrators of the persecution are the caciques and the local priests, both of whom have the most to lose when one of the villagers becomes an evangelical.

3. The primary reason for persecution is that a believer's conversion threatens the lifestyle and economic power of those holding the seat of authority.

4. Persecution is one of the great purifiers of the body of Believers in Christ.

5. The Gospel of the Lord Jesus Christ, when preached with the power of the Holy Spirit and lived in the same manner, carries within itself the seeds of confrontation with the rest of the world.

6. The Gospel of Jesus Christ is foreign to every culture. That does not mean that it destroys culture, but it does strip it of

ungodly elements, purifying it.

7. We should not be surprised that Christians are persecuted if they live out the Lordship of Jesus Christ in their lives, and refuse to bend to the influence of the world around them.

Church Historian Kenneth Scott LaTourette wrote, "So radical are the claims of the Gospel, so sweeping are its demands on the faithful, so uncompromising does it render those who yield themselves fully to it, that opposition and even persecution are to be expected."

More importantly, Jesus Christ told his first disciples, "Do not think that I have come to bring peace on earth; I have not come to bring peace, but a sword."[2] He clearly warned His disciples of the kind of opposition and confrontation they would encounter. Hostility and antagonism was to be the norm. He said, "In the world you will have tribulation."[3] Jesus knew then, and teaches us now, that "Men love darkness rather than light, because their deeds are evil. Everyone who does evil hates the light, and will not come to the light, for fear that his deeds will be exposed."[4] These words were almost a benediction: "They persecuted me, they will persecute you."

As night follows day, so persecution will follow God's Word when it is made available to a people in a language they can understand. This is powerfully illustrated in the life of a British believer born in 1330, by the name of John Wycliffe. The great challenge of Wycliffe's life was to make the Word of God available to the common man, getting the Bible and its message from the pulpit to the pew, from the church to the home, from the head to the heart. He would tell anyone who would listen that "God's word is what will give men new life, more than other words that are for pleasure." "Obviously, such miracles, he wrote, "could not be done by the work of a priest."

Wycliffe was himself a Bible scholar, and the more he studied it, the more he realized that in his own country, straying far from God's word had led to abuses by the church, and he began preaching publicly about those abuses.

Though his messages were religious, they were taken to be political, and the retribution against him began. He was deserted by his influential political friends, and lost his teaching post at Oxford University. As is often the case with Biblical persecution, it served as a spark which ignited the hearts of many of his students. They joined him in exile, and began the task of translating the Bible into English. Upon completion, copies were made, and his "poor preachers" began to take the Word to the common man.

Wycliffe succumbed to a stroke in 1384. The church condemned him, but his memory and influence continued to grow. He was later again officially condemned at the Council of Constance. The church and the government together gave orders that his writings were to be destroyed. His bones, so that they would not desecrate the sacred ground of his nation, were dug up and burned. His ashes were thrown unceremoniously into the river.

The officials of the church thought they were through with John Wycliffe forever. How wrong they were. They had not read from their own Bibles, if indeed any of them had one, the words of Jeremiah, "'Is my Word like a fire,' says the Lord, 'and like a hammer that breaks the rock in pieces?'" Today, the Wycliffe Bible translators and their peers continue in their passion to give God's Word to the Indians of Chiapas in their own language. They all realize the power of the Word comes at a great cost, yet the fruit is inevitable for the humble and teachable heart. Try as they might, the church could not destroy the vision of John Wycliffe, for it carried with it the power of the Word.

The translation of the Bible is a lifetime task. In 1969, Vern and Carla Sterk began as most evangelical missionaries to Mexico do. They moved with their children out to a small village. When food was in short supply, they went hungry like everyone else. When rains came, they were affected by the wet and cold the same as the others in the village. They shared the local diet and diseases, raised their family and translated the Bible into the native heart language of the Indians of the village.

In March 1998, in the village of Yavteclum, Chiapas, Mexico, there was a celebration. Five thousand bodies, heated with both excitement and the midday sun, churned on the mountainside. Rivulets of gravel roads emptied travelers from the canopy of surrounding jungle into the clearing. Jose watched in anxious fascination from his spot on the hastily assembled stage that looked so out of place in the rocky amphitheater. Sweat stained the collar of his freshly washed frock. His frock distinguished him as a catechist. In all the years that he had been riding his burro between the hidden highland villages, carrying doctrine from the cathedral to the commoners, Jose had never felt the strange combination of nausea and anticipation that now filled his stomach and lungs.

It was the day of the Bible dedication. To a hundred million other people in many parts of the world, "Bible" was a commonplace word that fit neatly in sentences about textbooks and Sundays. But to a man like Jose, a native of the Chenaloa tribe whose commonplace word is survival, "Bible" was a word that made his skin shiver, even on a sunny day. Jose had never actually read the words of God in his own language. His whole life was devoted to carrying the message of Jehovah to his native people, translating the character of God for them from Spanish into a language they could understand. Today was to be the day he would hear the Creator speak to him in the words of his own language.

Jose scanned the crowd. Soldiers in green uniforms, wielding sub-machine guns, patrolled the perimeter of the clearing, ever wary of the political time-bomb that ticked inside Chiapas. Just the week before, two more Indians had been murdered, and threats from every faction danced unspoken in the air. Electric blue and iridescent green ribbons and clothes laced the crowd, speaking the undeniable presence of the indigenous people. This day was for them.

Perhaps the most baffling to Jose was the awkward camaraderie between the Catholics and the Evangelicals. It was as if for one brief moment in time they had shelved their pulpit wars, their timeless battles, and their eternal disputes, and come together to see this miracle. Ten years of painstaking labor and united hours of grueling translation by a team of six, including Catholics, Evangelicals, Indigenous people, and American scholars. Together, these historical enemies had brought the greatest gift of all to the Tzotzil tribes of Mexico's forgotten corner; they brought the Book of Life.

Tense were the conversations that stirred the silence of the trees above. Then, above the discordant notes of the jumbled crowd, came a chord of shocking unity. Faces froze and turned to find the sound. Jose turned with them and dropped a heartbeat in the wonder of it. A choir.

One hundred and fifty voices joined in perfect harmony, lifting, soaring, grazing the sky with their beauty. This choir boasted no rich satin robes. Their voices were not refined with hours of training and years of practice. Their hands held no gold-paged hymnals, and their faces carried no rehearsed expressions of artistic holiness. But Jose was sure that in all of Rome's finest cathedrals, no music carried such intrinsic passion as the notes that filled the awe of silence in this moment.

Side by side the voices stood, here a farmer, there a vendor, men and women, Catholic and Evangelical, dark-skinned and mestizo, light-skinned and native, bright colors, black ties, pacifists and warriors, clergy and peasants . . . their song rose to touch the sky.

The song was over, but no one turned away. It was perfect.

A throat cleared, and someone undertook the awkward task of interrupting the silence. The welcome words were far away, and when the speaker turned to Jose, he was startled from his reverie. He brought his mind to focus. His was the task of translating the

words of the Spanish-speaking pastor into the Tzotzil language of
his people. Carefully, he followed the pastor through the welcome
speech, and introduced the bishop Don Samuel Ruiz. He struggled to stay with the Bishop's brief words of gratitude, for the
glory of the moment was overwhelming. Bishop Ruiz stepped
away from the podium, having kept the sacredness of the occasion
pure of any political references.

The pastor stood again. He opened his Spanish Bible to a passage in Isaiah, and began to read:

"Here is My Servant Whom I have chosen, the One I love, in
Whom I delight; I will put My spirit upon Him, and He will proclaim justice to the nations. He will not quarrel or cry out; no one
will hear His voice in the streets. A bruised reed He will not break,
and a smoldering wick He will not snuff out, till He leads justice
to victory. In His name, the nations will put their hope."

Hesitating, the pastor allowed Jose time to translate in
Tzotzil. Jose began the familiar words, then stopped. Turning to
the pastor, he stretched out his hand. "May I read it?" he asked.
The pastor reverently picked up the first and only printed copy of
the translated Bible, and passed it to Jose as if handling a newborn
child. Jose fingered the pages in his hands. Pure gold. He found
Isaiah and began, reading the words of the Lord off the page:

"Here is My Servant whom I have chosen, the One I love ..."
his voice broke, and the people waited expectantly. Even the soldiers at the edge of the circle seemed to pause and wait for Jose to
continue. Jose could not. The centuries of darkness were evapo-
rating in the brilliant sun of revelation, and left only a hot spring
of joy that broke upon his cheeks. It was as if he had been standing at a stained glass window, seeing the love of Christ through
the shaded panes of another language, another interpreter, another culture. Now, word by word, the panes of glass were breaking
and he was face to face with Lord Jehovah. Jose wept, and the
crowd wept with him.

Then a new voice filled his chest, and he continued. For the first time in all of history, the word of the Lord came to the Tzotzil people, from His mouth to their ears, in their own language:

"A bruised reed He will not break, and a smoldering wick He will not snuff out, until He leads justice to victory. In His name the nations will put their hope."

From above, the Creator looked on. And His heart filled with joy.

Joy laced the days and weeks that followed. The sun shone purer, now that Pasquala knew whose hand held it in place. The earth's womb seemed more fertile and gentler to her touch, as she pulled her stubborn hoe and created songs of worship to the Creator God.

The rooster still awoke her early in the morning, before the sun lent its glow to the mountain village. A scant banana did no more now to fill her aching belly in the morning than it had since that day the Jefe's men killed her mother. Each time the black of night began to fade, she stumbled through the trees and dipped her pail into the gaping well, then grappled with its heaviness every step to the hut and her sisters' thirsty impatience. None of this had changed.

But somehow, in between the blistered bites of the hoe's rough handle and the cramps of hunger, her mind found rest in the strong grip of Peace. No longer could the spirits haunt her. For the first time in all of her remembered life, she could go to sleep at night free from the phantoms' fear.

This, coupled with the lingering excitement of Gustavo's healing, left Pasquala and her young sisters craving more stories of Jehovah God. Agustino came to visit them, and told them all the stories he remembered. It was the dry summer season, and many days, when the sun blazed too fiercely to spend time weeding the field or carrying water to the wilting sprouts, Pasquala and her young sisters would walk to Agustino's hut and drink in the cool refreshment of his stories.

In her young imagination she walked the mountainsides with Jehovah-Rafa, as He touched the lepers' skin and healed their shame. She saw their eyes, once hidden behind a veil, now burn with the hope that the Healer offered, then burst into fires of wonder as their wounds closed and the veils fell away.

Her mind followed the Maker God through the smells of village markets, as He wove between the raucous vendors and the booths that overflowed with bright rainbows of pineapples, corn, melons and pomegranates. Joining the crowds of children that Agustino described, Pasquala saw Him lift a crippled man to his feet and send him dancing off in crazed amazement. She listened to the Master's stories, of rich men and beggars, lost coins and buried treasures, meals with pigs and great fiestas for all who would come.

Soon, Agustino had told them all he knew, for he was old, and his memory faltered beneath the weight of his years. But he told them of a man in San Cristobal, where Rosa took her bracelets and baskets to sell. This man, Miguel Cashlan, had a copy of the book where all the stories were found. He could read the Spanish language and translate the stories to Tzotzil, so Pasquala and her sisters would understand.

This brought great excitement to the girls. To see the book of stories for themselves, and hear more of the great Creator God, who rescued them from dreams, and had made the one great sacrifice, was worth a journey of any distance.

So it was that they began to walk the three-hour journey along the gravel road to San Cristobal every Sunday, while the villagers worshiped the spirits. Early in the morning, while the chill of night caused their bones to tremble and their feet to burn, Pasquala woke with the true enthusiasm of a thirteen-year-old girl. Packing bananas and tortillas in a sack, she led her sisters into the morning twilight and down the trail to town.

Miguel Cashlan would stand upon a corner of the center square and tell the gathering crowd of tourists, mestizos and village pilgrims the stories of the greatest God. He told them the words of Jehovah-Jesus, who said to love Creator God with all your heart and mind and soul and strength. Jehovah-Jesus said that anyone could come and taste the freedom of the truth He offered, and in all the simplicity of her youth, Pasquala knew the freedom Miguel Cashlan described.

While across the mountains and some kilometers away, other girls and boys of thirteen years donned elegant costumes and carelessly sprawled in the plushness of some cathedral's beauty, Pasquala rested aching feet on the bricks of the square and listened anxiously to the storyteller's voice, lest she miss a word and lose the message.

The square in San Cristobal filled with families and their children, drifting between the shady gardens that grew in the square's shadows. The sanitary white church spires poked menacingly at the skyline from one corner of the square, daring history to defy its claim to the souls of Mexico's children. Heavy wooden doors opened and closed several times as Cashlan spoke, changing shifts of faithful parishioners who came pay homage to the white-faced saints that posed inside the sanctuary.

Policemen cast furtive glances at the crowd gathered round Brother Cashlan, keeping up their sinister facade of reckless and relentless justice. Shoeshine boys stood at the fringes of the group, knowing there were few shoes to shine on the callused feet of this crowd. A crackpot pharmacist hawked his miracle cures for rheumatism or infertility from a respectful distance, as if he somehow sensed that the magic of Cashlan's message was greater than his own.

Time has rang past on the cathedral bells, yet no one left the crowd. Once, Cashlan stopped to ask for water and two or three small children raced to grant his request. It was all so new and fascinating, so different, yet so tantalizing. Even the youngest of Pasquala's sisters, who's seven years seemed hardly long enough to carry her the journey's length to town, was transfixed by the excitement of the characters Miguel described.

Late in the afternoon, when Miguel's voice cracked with tiredness, the girls would leave the square and trudge towards home. As the narrow walls of San Cristobal's streets spread wider into the open road to Chamula, they retold the stories time and time again. The words carved indelible pictures on their memories, and the character of Jehovah-Jesus grew to incomparable standing in their eyes.

While the trips to San Cristobal dropped them into an exhausted slumber upon their return to the dark solitude of their hut, the stories of Jehovah were their greatest contentment.

So it was that three months passed. Summer season reached its zenith, and the ground cracked like lizard skin. Pasquala crawled along the cycle of survival in the fashion of Indian destiny. Life seemed an endless wait for September's rains to come. Only Sunday's trips to San Cristobal broke the monotony of their impatience.

On a brilliant Sunday afternoon as July was ending, Pasquala trudged up the gravel road to San Juan Chamula, stretched between aching fatigue and the comfort of the messages Miguel had shared with her.

Today he read a story from Jehovah's book about a rich man who had a field of fertile soil. The rich man hired workers to plant the field and keep the weeds from eating the fruit that grew there. Unlike the jefe Pasquala remembered, this rich man was kind to his workers, treating them with fairness and respect. When the time came to harvest his field, the master sent a servant to the field to collect the fruit. But the workers of the field saw the servant coming and forgot their master's kindness, deciding they would keep the fruits of the harvest for themselves. So they beat the master's servant, humiliating him and sending him back to the master empty-handed. The master was very sad that his workers had behaved in this way. Wondering if they had misunderstood, he sent a second messenger to collect the harvest from the field he owned. Again, the wicked workers saw the messenger from a distance, and beat him severely when he arrived, sending him crawling back to the master's house. The master wept to see his servant treated in this way, and paced the floor in troubled dilemma. Because his heart was kind and merciful, he chose to give the workers one more chance.

"I know," he thought, "I'll send my only son. Then of course they will respect him and send me the fruit of the harvest."

So he sent his only son. The workers saw him in the distance. "Come," they said, "let's kill the Master's son. Then the harvest will be ours, and we will no longer be in service to anyone."

When the son arrived to bring the harvest to his father, the workers of the field met him at the gate. They mocked him abused him, and then they took him out and killed him. This was the way the workers of the earth treated the servants of the kind master.

Miguel told Pasquala how the master was the Creator God. The children of the Creator God are not liked by the other workers of the earth, who do not know the Master, and live in service to other spirits. That day, Miguel told Pasquala how the servants of Yajval Balamil would not like her for her loyalty to the Creator God. Jehovah-Jesus said His servants would suffer, but that they must continue to fast and pray, and He would be with them.

All these words churned in Pasquala's mind, as she rounded the final curve of her journey home. A noise from the bushes broke through her thoughts and brought her to a stop.

"Pasquala?" came the muffled voice, weak and slurred. It was Aunt Marta, the healer. The drunken healer. Pasquala shivered as she recognized the body, curled in a heap of dark wool and bright embroidery. Never since the day of her childhood, when her aunt spilled the chicken's blood to barter for her soul, could Pasquala meet the murky void in her aunt's eyes without a coldness creeping into her spirit. The woman lay by the roadside, reeking of posh. Kneeling beside her, she offered her hand to the woman's bony grip, and helped her find her balance. "Pasquala...girl," she stumbled through the thickness of her words, "help your auntie find her way."

The peace of today's journey vanished in the presence of this woman. Only an inkling of the fear so long defeated threatened to penetrate the wall Pasquala had been building.

"Pasquala," her aunt continued, causing Pasquala to tilt her nose towards the other shoulder to avoid the damp stagnation of the alcohol-soaked breath. "I know where you have been this day, child."

Pasquala answered her with silence.

"You know," she slurred heavily, "the people have been talking about you and your sisters, and they say that you haven't been to pray or light the candles for many days." She struggled through the accusation in the breathy effort of her condition.

Pasquala felt the sharpened grip of her aunt's arm slung about her shoulder, and the weight of darkness troubled her for breath. The fear threatened to break through the wall of certainty that guarded her new life, and then she stopped. She remembered. The water of belief that drowned her doubts the afternoon Gustavo came back to them alive filled her chest and set afloat the weight of fear that pressed her shoulders.

"Yes, auntie." She confessed the truth. "We have learned of a great new God called Jehovah-Rafa, and we now pray to Him."

Fear shriveled up and cowered back into the corner, and Pasquala continued on the path home.

"I've heard this story, and the spirits tell me they're angry." The voice of her aunt tipped with uneasiness.

"You will be at the fiesta?" Aunt Marta asked the question with the tone of a command, and the girl was uncertain whether it was a request or a threat.

"I cannot go, aunt. The fiesta honors spirits we no longer worship. Besides, we cannot give our money for the posh, and the drunkenness gives me fear that I no longer want.

"Well then!" her aunt erupted angrily, letting go of Pasquala's shoulder and stepping unsteadily out on her own. "Perhaps you had better be careful with yourself!"

She leaned in conspiratorially towards Pasquala's small cheek. "The villagers have two gallons of gasoline and some say they are going to burn your house down!" They know of your unfaithfulness, and the gods are angry!"

Having delivered her ominous warning, the healer wove distance between herself and her rebellious niece, climbing up a side path to her home. Pasquala stood for a moment, watching the bent old woman lurch up the rocky path, digesting the secret that drunkenness had loosed. The sky above was spreading its carpet for the parade of stars that night would bring, and she hurried the last half kilometer to her hut.

Her sisters had stayed home, too weak from yesterday's sun to make the long trip to San Cristobal. Tortillas, chile peppers and some corn where spread out on the little table, awaiting her return.

"Pasquala!" Her sisters danced around her, laughing in relief that the loneliness had lifted and their protectress had returned. Pasquala was their hero. Besides, the skinny thirteen-year-old girl who ran the house was their provider and mother. Pasquala laughed with them, still no more than a child herself. They pulled crates up to the table and sat down together, still giggling in the silliness of youth.

Pasquala picked at the food before her. Hunger escaped her. She watched the young girls inhale their corn and chilies, having waited hours for Pasquala to return. Pasquala became distracted by a cockroach that scuttled from the doorway light into the shadows of the wall.

"Eat, Pasquala," urged the youngest, so proud of her own contribution to the dinner preparations.

"This Friday is the fiesta," Pasquala stated, as if just remembering. The other girls kept eating, seemingly unaffected by the news. Even though Pasquala had no appetite, their enthusiasm didn't suffer. Careful not to spill a single kernel, they scooped corn onto the tortillas and packed bites into their mouths with the tiny hands that belonged to Tzotzil children.

Swallowing her last mouthful, Pasquala's sister answered the extraneous remark with another random reminder. "Aunt Rosa is bringing her daughter tomorrow to stay with us for the week while she goes to the coast."

Rosa was a fairly skilled artisan, and would dig clay from the riverbank to make a few dozen pots to sell to the plantation owners in the lowlands. Pasquala could not understand how Rosa was able to sell her wares to the plantation bosses, knowing what they had done to her mother, but that was Rosa's affair. Besides, Rosa often paid her a small amount for minding her two daughters. Pasquala needed the money, especially after the way this dry season had left much of the corn in their small field wilted and worthless.

Pasquala could refrain no longer. Mother protector or not, she was no more than a child herself, and the strain of the conversation with Aunt Marta was more than she could bear alone. In a controlled torrent, she let the encounter fall out onto the table among the remaining crumbs of her uneaten dinner.

"I saw Aunt Marta today." With the words came fear, and with fear out in the open, her tears followed. "She was drunk, and began asking me why we don't buy candles or come to church anymore."

Silence stilled the two younger girls, who sensed Pasquala's urgency.

"She told me the spirits are angry with us for worshipping the Creator God, and that many of the villagers are angry, too." With this, her tears turned to sobs. As if it wasn't isolated enough to live with two young sisters, no father, and only a pleasant memory of her mother. Now the villagers had turned against them, and she hadn't even known it.

"She said the villagers bought gasoline from San Cristobal, and may burn our house down to appease the spirits and punish us for our unfaithfulness to the gods."

The other girls left the crates they sat on and huddled protectively around Pasquala. So often, only children possess the sensitivity of silence; both children simply held their sister. Her tears dampened their dusty shirts and made little mud smears on her face where the dirt and water met. The youngest stroked Pasquala's long black braids, toying with the brightly colored ribbons at the end in quiet comfort, until the shudders of emotion subsided. It was she who spoke first.

"Creator God will be with us." She was only seven. She had never read a Bible for herself, nor was there a Bible printed in her language. She didn't go to church, she didn't memorize a prayer. She didn't know the ten commandments, didn't understand hypocrisy, didn't have theology. In the simplistic purity of a child's faith, she knew the answer. Fear did not have a hold on her. Threats of disaster, of revenge, of destruction of the only material possessions she had on this earth did not ripple the ocean of faith this child possessed.

Faith stood up against the fear that had begun to invade the room, and drove it backwards. Pasquala stopped crying, and basked in the peace she had almost forgotten. Of course. Creator God would be with them. The One who was greater than all gods. The three young children of God held onto each other in the middle of the hut, on the edge of town, high in the mountains of Chiapas.

THE SWORD OF

CHANGE

THE CROSS OF

EVERYDAY LIFE

Chapter 6

No one puts a piece of unshrunk cloth on an old
garment; for the patch pulls away from the garment,
and the tear is made worse. Nor do people
put new wine into old wineskins, or else the wineskins break, the
wine is spilled, and the wineskins are ruined.
But they put new wine into new wineskins,
and both are preserved.

Matthew 9:16-17

THE SWORD OF CHANGE

A double edged sword can cut in both directions. The Roman Catholics in Chiapas are feeling the sword of change for the first time in their history there, as the Catholic population decreases - along with the power of the Catholic Church.

Mexico has been well-near 100 percent Catholic for several hundred years. Therefore, every Protestant conversion represents a net loss for the Catholic church.

Stemming the tide of defections to Protestantism was the primary topic on Pope Paul II's agenda when he met with the Roman Catholic bishops of Latin America in October, 1990. Meeting together to celebrate the 500-year anniversary of Columbus' arrival in the New World, the discussion was not of Columbus, and certainly not of Chiapas' first Bishop, Bartolome de las Casas, but rather of a so-called new Evangelization, "a phrase," according to David Miller of NNI, "expressing their commitment to a vigorous strategy to preach the gospel more effectively in the Hispanic world." Their hope was to reverse the serious decline in their church membership in the region.

It hasn't worked. Statistics reveal the Roman Catholic flock is steadily shrinking in this historic bastion. Miller reports, "Though Roman Catholic membership grew by 30 million in the past decade, the general population increased by nearly 80 million." At issue was what had happened to the 50 million people that they could in past decades have assumed were theirs. Failure to keep pace with population growth, especially for a church that inducts members automatically through infant baptism, signifies a net decline and activates more than one panic button.

There was little comfort for the visiting Pope in being told that the percentage of professing Catholics in the general population had dropped eleven percent during the 1980's, and that they were losing the "near absolute allegiance" they once enjoyed, but had not protected. The Mexican bishops, meeting two years later, had at the top of their agenda "The rapid growth of Protestantism in Mexico." They were terribly concerned when they saw that nearly twenty million people, roughly a quarter of the population, had become Protestant.

Presbyterian evangelist Calo Fabio D'Araujo says the process in Brazil, like Mexico, was that the "Catholic Church lost itself and the soul of the country to the voodoo cults many years ago.

They have been losing people to these cults for years, but it never bothered them because the cults don't ask for total and absolute loyalty, as the evangelicals do. It is possible to be a Catholic in a voodoo cult." It is not uncommon for many people to profess both religions. In one church in Brazil, sixty percent of the members profess to belong to both a voodoo cult and to the Catholic Church. The church is known as "Black Rome."

Though syncretism is not as rampant in Mexico as in Brazil, there are still noticeable conversions from Christopaganism (being both Catholic and animist). The statistics, however, simply designate them as "converts from the Catholic faith," while in reality they might have been actual animists or members of any number of sects, but were baptized, married, and buried in the Catholic order.

The increase in Protestantism in Mexico parallels what is happening all over Latin America. Statistics indicate that Evangelical Christian churches, which were non-existent in Latin America a century ago, are establishing themselves in force. Miller reports, "During the 1980's, the total Protestant population increased from 18.6 million to 59.4 million. That represents a whopping 220 percent growth rate, nine times the rate of increase in general population. The rapid proliferation of the evangelicals, as Protestant Christians are commonly known, has promoted observers to dub the 1980's as the 'decade of the Protestant Reformation in Latin America.'"

Historians draw intriguing comparisons with the 16th century. One suggestive statistic: the defection of Roman Catholics to Protestant churches has been quantitatively greater in Latin American in the last ten years than it was in Central Europe in the days of Martin Luther. Little wonder the Pope registered strong disapproval of the Protestant's aggressive evangelism, and urged his Latin American brethren to defend the faith against what the peace-loving Pope called "rapacious wolves."

Actually, the thousands of Catholics that are converting to Protestantism in Latin America are doing so for the same reasons many of the Indians are converting in Chiapas. The reason so many are converting has not so much to do with politics, as we are led to believe, but with culture. It is bound up with the Indian's spiritual quest for a personal God. "People are awakening to a new vision," says a former priest. "The world has changed, and the Catholic church has stayed behind with its traditions, bottled up, closed in. The church has not kept up-to-date in terms of presenting a message to today's world. All their lives, Catholics have had this image of a dead Christ, a Christ who is born to them as a child in December, is crucified at Holy Week and who remains in the tomb. For the majority of our Latin American people, Christ has not risen. On the other hand, the evangelical church has taken up the task of presenting a living Christ, a Christ of power that saves and heals. And interest is awaking amongst the people to know this living Christ."

Federico Bertuzzi, director of Argentina's interdenominational research and consulting agency, (COMIBAM) agrees: "The immense majority (of Latinos) are nominally Catholic, but they have never had an experience in the profound theological sense. It is common to find among nominal Catholics, persons who say to me, 'I like the way you evangelicals are. The pastor is married with a family. I like the way you visit one another.'"

"Some abandon the Catholic Church," says Bertuzzi, "because they have discovered a spiritual vacuum that has not ever been filled, no matter how much they have gone to Mass or talked with a priest. There is discontent, because they perceive the priest to be aloof from the people. When the priest does try to get next to the people he uses very political language and that doesn't satisfy them either."

The Western press is also taking note of the gain of the Protestants. John Richard Neuhaus wrote as early as 1990 on the phenomenon of Protestant growth in Mexico, "Whereas being Catholic is often a nominal factor in the Mexican cultural package, the Evangelical converts tend to be better educated, harder working, and eager to evangelize their fellow citizens. . . It is likely that Roman Catholics are already a minority in some states of Mexico."

Bishop Javier Lozano Barranga of Zacatecos lashes out, "The Yankees are interested in changing the mentality of the Mexican. That is why they are starting with the most profound, their religious mentality. The sects (i.e. Evangelicals) are the vanguard of an effort to change Mexican culture."

Leaders of the Roman Catholic Church in Mexico are accusing the Evangelicals of being a "new" front for "the CIA, the Rockefellers, and other masters of Yankees imperialism."

Not all Catholics in the U.S. agree. John O'Sullivan, editor of National Review, offers a different perspective. "I am a Catholic," says O'Sullivan, "so I have to have mixed feelings about the growth of Protestantism in Latin America. But these people get up in the morning, they go to work, they take care of their children, and they're faithful to their wives. So I expect that, all in all, the growth of Protestantism is a good thing for Latin America." Nationally Syndicated columnist Michael Novak, also a Catholic, has long held the view that Latin America needs a strong dose of what Max Weber called the Protestant (meaning Calvinist) work ethic. What they all appear to be saying is: the Reformation has now reached reached Latin America, and it is not a bad thing, for the country or the people.

The Pope would not agree. After the 1990 Papal visit to Mexico, there was reportedly a wake of intolerance towards all who were non-Catholic, namely Evangelicals, all of whom were former Catholics.

Elizabeth Isais, of New Network Internationals, reported: "Following the visit of Roman Catholic Pope John Paul II to Mexico, columnist Alvaro Cepeda Neri of Mexico City's daily La Jornada, concluded among other things that the pope "left a wake of intolerance against other churches and a diabolic scorn against the sects who approach the poor."

As the dust settled following the Pope's departure, many

evangelical leaders concluded that a major cause for the Prelate's visit was to stress Roman Catholicism as the only true church, and to persuade evangelicals (referred to as sects) to return to the Catholic fold.

In the southeastern state of Tabasco, where recent statistics indicate that well over ten percent of the population is evangelical, the Pope emphasized that Catholicism would welcome Evangelical converts back with open arms.

Columnist Utaco Pina, writing in the newspaper La Extra, titled one column "Why did the pope forget the Bible?" He wrote, "Never, among the countless messages that he delivered, did the Pope refer to the Book of books for Catholics: the Sacred Bible. . . We did not hear him quote the Psalms nor passages from the Gospels. He spoke only in passing about spirituality, instead centering his energies on political and social aspects. . . We consider that a grave mistake because many believers were disheartened to see a pope who is more political than mystical; a maximum authority of the church speaking about everything except ecclesiastical matters."

Editorial writer Enrique Alvarez Palacios, in the magazine Novedades, compared the Apostle Paul to the present pope, concluding, "Two colossus, of different time and character; two distinct servants of Christ. Saint Paul, pegged to original and eternal Christianity. His Holiness John Paul II, adhering to the political, economic and humanitarian needs of his time."

For months in advance of the Pope's visit, press, television and radio reports carried a myriad of speculations on what he would accomplish and where he would go. After his arrival on May 6, the media dedicated literally thousands of pages and hours to papal information. Though well-documented, the Pope's visit drew fire from a skeptical Mexican press, in some cases mirroring official disapproval of a politically involved church.

During the papal visit, a full-page ad in Mexico City's premier newspaper, El Excelsior, paid for by eleven associations of

Catholic cattlemen in the southern state of Chiapas, presented the pope with a series of nine "concerns," including the following:

"That the Catholic clergy is accomplice, by action or omission, of the violations of human rights that are committed by means of the expulsions that the indigenous people make against their brothers who form part of other churches or sects, but who do not consume alcohol, which is in conflict with the brotherhood and goodwill to which the church convokes all men on earth."

Another point in the declaration: "Today we can affirm that the Catholic church is linked with groups of small-time chiefs that manipulate the monopoly of aguardiente (liquor) and [soft drinks], an infamous alliance that the Holy See ought to be informed about, condemn and eradicate."

The manifest concluded with various petitions, one of which requested "that the violation of human rights on the part of the political clergy cease, not only in the fomentation of alcoholism, but also in the expulsions or invasions of lands."

In what appeared to be a response to the cattlemen's concerns, the pope addressed these specific points of the manifest, demanding an end to the excessive consumption of alcohol and, according to eyewitnesses, reading portions of scripture to at least one gathering during his visit to Chiapas, contrary to some reports in the Mexican press.

A church that has had 500 years to prove itself, and failed at most turns, has this telling indictment, given by a former Catholic priest, Alvaro Cadavid:

"Since childhood, I have had a desire to be involved in the things of God. The experience that moved me to serve the Lord was seeing the need of so many people that were far away from the Christian life. In Colombian communities our mentality is that, if someone wants to serve God, he or she much become a priest or nun and join the clerical establishment.

By 1972, the Catholic charismatic renovation movement had developed great strength. Being a university student at the time, I received a tremendous impact from my acquaintance with this movement. I saw there a moving of God that was different from what the traditional, rigid and structured church is. Even though the charismatic renovation seemed to me a little bit evangelical, nevertheless it was extraordinary. I could see the power of God in this movement.

I went on studying theology in the university. My goal was to become a priest. Once I was ordained, I had to do that which is one's obligation to do. I became a parish priest, celebrating Mass every day, administering the responsories, the rosaries, the images - everything involved in the day-to-day life of the people. Soon those renovating experiences of the Pentecostal movement died in me.

After some years in the religious life, a desire awoke in me to achieve something deeper in my life. The memories of what I had experience in my student days came to mind, so I returned once more to the charismatic renovation.

I got involved a bit with this movement and I started finding deeper things in the Word of God. I had matured by now in regard to my thinking about what the Bible says. I began to realize that certain things within my church did not fit very well with the Word of God.

I began to preach a bit differently from what I had before, pointing out certain things to people in light of the Bible; for example, the worship of images in my church. By carefully analyzing Exodus 20, I discovered the Word says you shall not honor them. I said that it was foolish to believe in these things. Little by little I did away with this custom. It is a form of superstition on the part of the people.

It used to disappoint me a lot to see so many persons arrive for communion at my church in a drunken state. Couples would come for the wedding and sometime the groom would have had too many drinks. He had been having his firewater in order to have the courage to tell the bride that he accepted her as his wife.

I started to see that within the church there needed to be a purification. One of the ways I chose to do that was by presenting a new message in light of the Word of the Lord.

So then the people began to say: the father is becoming evangelical. He is no longer in agreement with the things we are used to doing around here. Their comments eventually reached the Bishop.

The four years I was in the Catholic charismatic renovation were years of great internal struggle. I understood that I needed something new for my life, something beyond the rites of the Catholic Church. When one comes to understand things from another point of view, he must be sincere before God. The final crisis commenced in 1985.

I was leading some prayer groups here in the city. One night a leader of one of the groups invited me to a meeting. We went to the place and I found myself at the door of an evangelical church, the Assemblies of God Christian Center.

I had never been a friend of the evangelicals. Never. On the contrary, I hated them. In one Cauca village I had even threatened them with police action. As far as I was concerned, they were second-class people, the worst that could exist.

But when I entered that Christian Center, I began to experience something new. I found myself among a people that worshiped God. I found something very special, something very lovely. That began to have an impact on my life.

Two months later this same charismatic leader invited me to another meeting at the Christian Center. It was a service of the Lord's Supper. I had never experienced what the Lord's Supper was, but in that service the Lord spoke to my life through the preaching, the hymns, the praises. When the pastor gave the invitation to accept Christ as Lord and Savior, I wanted to do that. In my pew where I was I prayed: 'Lord, I open the door of my heart. Come in. Make me the person you want me to be.'

Well, from then on my life was turned completely upside down. It might be possible for some persons with a heart to serve God to remain in the Catholic church. But for a priest it is not possible. Being a leader in the church, the priest is obligated to lead the processions, to burn incense to images or to celebrate Mass for the dead. For a leader, therefore, it is not easy to maintain a Christian attitude.

At the end of 1986, they sent me to the Cauca valley so that I would not be in an environment where I would be in danger of absorbing evangelical ideas. Then, in 1988, the principal bishop of the charismatic renovation here in Colombia, Monsignor Alfonso Uribe Jaramillo, called me in and said that I must make a decision to be either Catholic or Protestant.

He did not know what to do with me. Everybody was saying I had Protestant ideas. I answered him that the Protestants were more correct in the way they expounded the things of God.

The bishop started to get upset with me. He told me to keep quiet and then sent me to another town. I lasted two more years there, struggling the whole time.

It was when I had to celebrate a Mass for Saint

Lazarus that I realized that I would definitely have to leave the church. He is a personage listed in the Central American canon of saints. They give him a lot of devotion; even the witches invoke the name of Saint Lazarus in their work. The celebration of that Mass disturbed me a great deal because I found myself involved in something so empty, something that made no sense.

That is when I really started to think. I could not go on. A few days later I wrote a letter to the bishop in which I told him that I had decided to leave.

I began working with Jesus Medina, a (Protestant) pastor in Bucaramanga. There I took my first definite steps in the Christian life. Some four months later I was baptized in water. After that I wrote the bishop once more and told him that I had definitely decided to abandon Roman Catholicism.

Every day there are priests that come to know the Word of the Lord and, as a result, questions are raised in their minds. I know there are many priests that are not in agreement with what they are doing in their church. They have started awakening to reality."

It is not only the priests that are beginning to do what a few years ago was unthinkable. The much-hated caciques are not beyond the reach of the "risen and alive Christ."

Manuel San Juan exudes strength and quiet confidence. His home has become a house church this Sunday morning, as sounds of praise and worship fill the air. It was not always this way. As a former cacique, the tribal bullies who often persecute evangelicals, Manuel was no friend of the Christians.

Manuel shares about his conversion to Christianity. The incredible change took place in September 1995.

"When we gathered together for our civic meetings," recalls Manuel, "the municipal president incited us by stating that the evangelicals were burning Catholic churches. In private, he used to tell us that since he couldn't sell them beer anymore, it proved the Gospel was a bad influence."

Juan Perez, an evangelical Christian, shared the Gospel with Manuel for more than a year. "I did not beat him over the head with a Bible," Perez explains. "I just talked to him, prayed to God and become a friend." Eventually Manuel, a striking man in his late 50s, who has authority over some 40,000 people in the area, asked the Lord into his heart.

Manuel is often asked by his former friends about the changes in his life, which he is quick to share. "But not everyone asks or tries to understand," he says. Manuel was recently fired upon as he drove home. When he heard the shots, he realized that some leaders wanted him dead.

"I will not be bullied into disobeying God. If they want me, I am here. But it is obvious that God also wants me here. My life is in His hands."

"This is my property," he continues, while songs of praise float softly in the background. "More than that, it is God's property. This is the place where I want to build a church for all the people in these communities. In Jesus Christ, all things are possible."[1]

*Then many false prophets will rise up and deceive many. And
because lawlessness will abound, the love of many will grow cold.
But he who endures to the end shall be saved.*

Matthew 24:11-13

*If anyone desires to come after Me, let him deny himself, and take
up his cross, and follow Me.*

Matthew 16:24

THE CROSS OF EVERYDAY LIFE

Jesus Christ said, "Take up your cross daily and follow me."
Like so much of scripture, this concept is easier to give as an
injunction to others than to apply to one's own situation.

The Indians of Chiapas' shoulders are calloused from their
heavy, daily crosses, crosses they are forced to bear alone. For
many Chiapas Indians, the cross of the future is as dark and heavy
as the cross of the past five hundred years. It is as sliver-ridden,
blood-stained, and nail-pierced as it has ever been.

As they make their trek through everyday life there are a few
words of comfort spoken to them, such as, "I will liberate you, I
will get your land back, I will free you from the tyranny of the
politicians, I will restore your culture, I will supply you with
weapons." But somehow, the promises are at best short rest stops
on another day's hopeless journey.

Daily life is a cross that is to be borne without complaint and
without hope, with memories of unkept promises and dissipated
expectation. Seen from a distance, their life may have an aura of

peace, gentleness and natural beauty, like the deceptively tranquil village of Tila. The sloping hills, the banana grove and the quietness speak of tranquillity. The church, sitting on the high hill overlooking the town, with its muted red and yellow trim, and its traditional loud speakers mounted on each side of the cross, rises above all the other structures in Tila, suggesting hope, safety, order, and justice.

This picturesque scene is as deceptive as the promises that have been made to the Indians and soon broken, as in so many other villages carved out of the wilderness.

The typical welcome to the village can be a prelude of what to expect there. Out of the bushes, young men, armed with an array of weapons appear, throwing a long, spike-embedded strap across the road. They want money. No one smiles, they just finger their carbines and machetes. A first offering is not enough. After it is increased, a surly young man takes it, nods, and another steps forward to remove the spikes. Not sure of the signal, you smile nervously and drive on. Looking back, the young men have disappeared into the bushes to wait for the next visitor.

Entering the village as the sun starts to recede, the shadow of a cross slowly moves across the city square. There are no children laughing, no open markets, only a few men sitting drinking, with their machetes or guns at their side. There are no smiles of greeting, only frigid looks of practiced distrust and disdain as you look for a place to buy a soda.

Two hours away, in San Cristobal, one may be greeted by a smile, and offered the "coldest drink in the city." Little children look up from the floor to smile, and then return to their coloring books. Not here. The children peek cautiously around corners. All of the faces ask the same thing: Who are these people and whose side are they on? Are they trouble?

Tila is a town divided. Facing the city square at one end of the street is the Catholic church, the PRD (Party of the Democratic Republic), and the Zapatistas. Together they proclaim "liberty to the poor," "freedom to the oppressed," and "justice for injustice."

At the other end of the street are their opponents. They are the PRI, the official ruling party of Mexico, the AbyXu, named after the red night ant with its vicious sting, and the Paz y Justice (Development, Peace and Justice) Party. They all share two things in common: their certainty of the righteousness of their cause, and their loaded and cocked weapons.

Caught inside their struggle are the Indians, moving with caution to purchase or sell the necessary supplies for daily existence, careful not to be at the wrong place at the wrong time.

As the church bells ring, people slowly leave their homes and cross the square to the church. No one speaks. This is only a momentary truce between enemies. All listen to Father Heriberto Cruz Vera, who stands in his pulpit dressed in white robes, shouting a message that blares through loud speakers to those inside and outside the church, "The world neo-liberalism, where the poor don't count is a puppet of death." He compares his church with that of the early church. "The early Christians," he thunders, "were savagely persecuted by the Roman Empire, but they eventually conquered the state and transformed the world. Today, it is our duty to again transform the world."

At the end of the street another preacher, Marcos Albino, not a professed "liberation theologian" but a city councilman for the ruling Institutional Revolution Party, the PRI, 32-years old, portly, a former Mexican army corporal and without the benefit of loudspeakers explains, "Father Cruz Vera is doing Satan's work, preparing people to kill. He has been blessing their weapons with candles and killing black chickens, using their blood to bless the carbines so they work. It is black magic." Though Albino is himself a practicing Catholic, (communion is sometimes withheld from him) he says his bishop, Bishop Ruiz, "wants to be the father of the Indians, but a diabolical father."

Life on the front line in Tila is much different than in the city of San Cristobal, where civil rights activists from Europe and the

U.S. get off their air conditioned buses to buy Marcos T-shirts, Zapatista dolls, and stickers saying, "I Love Marcos." In the city streets, the crosses dangle around necks on gold chains.

Everyone in Tila knows that just one person, saying the wrong thing, or one bullet aimed at the wrong person, can trigger world headlines, as it did in the small neighboring village of Acteal. Acteal also had its church, its cross, and its loudspeakers, but there was also another, very different, building near the outskirts of town. Several hundred residents, many of them refugees from military action in other cities, gathered in it, to pray that God would intervene and keep them safe. It was an Evangelical church. Its members had run out of all options. The "Evangelicals" in this case, and in others as well, included both Protestants and Catholics. Their commonality is in believing in the Lord Jesus Christ, and following Him as the Lord of their lives.

While they were praying one afternoon, a column of gunmen descended secretly into the village and onto the church. Without warning, they opened fire on the church with their AK47s. One survivor told correspondents, "We were there praying for peace when I first heard the shots. Everyone began running in every direction. Families were separated. As we ran for the mountainside for cover they followed us and shot many of us." Many were gunned down on the banks of a river below the town. Radio reports indicated that "the attackers wiped out whole families in apparent random shootings." One cried, "We escaped the terror from our home village, and now look what has happened here. Where can we go next?"

The attackers, wearing ski masks and red bandanas, disappeared into the trees, leaving behind 45 dead, including eleven women. President Ernesto Zedillo went on national television to call the massacre "an absurd criminal act," but that was of little comfort to 15-year-old Juan Vazques Luna, who fearfully made his way back to the church, crying out to God, "Why?" as he dug the graves to bury his mother, father and four sisters.

This massacre, on December 22, 1997, was a warning to the people of Acteal, and a prophecy for Tila and many other villages in Chiapas. It followed a pattern that began in the 1960's of believers being harassed and expelled from their villages by traditional Indian religionists, who have long controlled village life. These traditional religionists are animist Catholics, Christopagans, and members of the PRI, the ruling party in Mexico for the last 70 years. The local party bosses of each village, the caciques, insist they be allowed autonomous operation. Local and state government officials, in order to not lose the votes of the village, do not normally intervene when the caciques kill or expel evangelicals.

The Evangelicals at Acteal burying their dead, those hiding on the mountain, and those waiting in dread in Tila know they may become the newest additions to an estimated 20,000 Christian Indian refugees within the state of Chiapas. The massacred forty-five at Acteal joined an unknown number of people already martyred for their faith. Their number is estimated in the hundreds. Refugees expelled from a village because of their faith in Christ lose all of their possessions and their right of land usage. Many end up in the city of San Cristobal. It is their children who sell the "quaint" souvenirs to the Human Rights activists and tourists sitting in the city park drinking beer, and enjoying a bit of "native hospitality."

Sometimes the government will be persuaded to give the dispossessed evangelicals a piece of land on which to build a new village. The donated land, however, is very restricted in size, so the refugee families are never really able to recover their old way of life.

The Zapatista regime has introduced politics into the situation. The Catholic clergy of the region, like Father Vera, who have adopted liberation theology and openly support armed resistance, now side with the Zapatistas, or at least favor their supposed goals. Many Indians follow the Catholic clergy's Liberation Theology, which does not preclude overt violence to "free the poor." Many Indians become Zapatistas through the encouragement of their local priests, clinging to their promises about bettering their situation. This inevitably brings the military into the situation, whose job it is to stop all violence, by force if necessary.

Human rights organizations are fairly diligent in reporting the political and sociological abuses that are taking place in Chiapas. One does not have to travel very far outside San Cristobal to verify they they are reporting truthfully. One such appraisal, from Human Rights Watch, is titled, Implausible Deniability: State Responsibility for Rural Violence in Mexico. This report is unique in that it not only deals with the "political" and "sociological" aspects of Chaipas, but also includes this report on religious persecution: "Though still predominately Catholic, the Mexican population is increasingly turning to evangelical Protestantism. As many as twenty million Mexicans are estimated to belong to evangelical churches. . . In Chiapas, says CON-FRATERNICE President, Arturo Farela, some 1,000,000, or just over 25 percent of the population are evangelical. . . While Catholic-evangelical conflicts have led to violence and expulsions in the state, many of the conflicts also have political or economic roots. In a special report on the issue, the CNDH (Comision Nacional de Derechos Humanos) documented the expulsion from their communities of some 15,000 evangelicals in 132 cases, between 1966 and 1993. The CNDH found support for the hypothesis that people viewed as 'troublemakers' (i.e. Evangelicals) were expelled, including 'modern Catholics' (Catholics who remained Catholics but became evangelicals.)"

This aspect of human rights abuse is rarely, if ever, reported by Human Rights organizations, the news media, or the internet new services. It is just one more cross to be borne by evangelical Indians - that of suffering alone.

The Chols, as pointed out by Dr. Henry Aulie, don't become instant saints upon conversion, any more than in other cultures. They tend to lack self-consciousness and self-occupation.

Basically, they all think alike. Their poverty, though, has spared them from confusing "wants" with "needs." They are content to have family and kin around them, if together they could wrest a living from the soil. This same, simple contentment's downside is apathy and fatalism, which can lead to neglect and irresponsibility in important matters.

They are unwilling to see others, even their own kin, rise to a social level above the community. Due to this peer pressure, the only recourse for an ambitious young person is to reject their Indian culture, and adopt that of the mestizo. Doing so brings resentment and criticism from his family. Many of the young will admire him, however, secretly hoping to follow.

Nevertheless, as they accept Jesus Christ as Lord of their lives, the changes that God brings are far-reaching. Aulie reports, "Where the saving work of God has been thoroughly done," (through evangelism and discipleship) "Indians seems to have an intuitive insight into the changes that must be made. They recognize that old practices having religious significance must go, while folklore, or customs not involving moral or religious issues, may be retained. They themselves tend to drop old customs without being prompted by the missionaries. Although believers have the mind of their culture on matters that do not conflict with the Word of God, at the same time they recognize they are to have the mind of Christ, which may be discerned in the written scripture in their own language."

There is a noticeable difference between Christopagans, who practice both Roman Catholicism and paganism, and Evangelicals, who have put their faith in Jesus Christ and the Word of God. This is graphically seen in the differences between a testimony given by a Christopagan who called himself a Christian, and the sermon of an Evangelical Chol.

"I was sick," said the Christopagan. A shaman came and took my pulse and told me I was suffering from a serious disease. 'I'll come back tomorrow to cure you,' he said. 'Tell them to bring wax candles, tallow candles,

copal resin, a liter of posh, a rooster, and some flowers.'
I knew this was how people were cured in our village, but
I didn't understand why. That night my mother and my
wife were talking about our troubles, and I heard them.
Then I understood about the curing.

Each one of us has a spirit, which is an animal that
lives in the mountains and represents us in every way.
When the spirit is fat and contented from eating well, its
owner is healthy too. But when it can't find enough to eat
in the woods, or when it's frightened or it falls into a
canyon, then its owner gets sick.

The spirit of a shaman is wiser and more able, and
that is why it takes care of our spirits. The spirit of a
shaman is called a petome or saclome. The duty of the
petomes and saclomes to take care of our spirits is given
to them by Chultotic (one of their gods). But they have
to be coaxed to protect us. That's why the shaman drinks
posh when he's going to work a cure, because the spirits
like to drink.

Some of the spirits in the mountains are stronger
than ours, and they catch them and eat them. They're the
pukujes and the kibales, which are the spirits of the war-
locks. If they catch a weak spirit, its owner gets sick and
if they eat it he dies."

Contrast that story with this sermon, preached by an evangelical church elder, who has "become a new creature in Christ;
old things have passed away and all things have become new." He
is a Chol, culturally, but a Christian, spiritually.

"The government uses men to speak to us. God also
uses men. The Word does not come to us on the wind
but through men. Long ago God spoke to the Israelites,
our predecessors, through the prophets. Those are the
ones who had the privilege of preaching. But the
Israelites did not believe. The prophets predicted that a

Savior would come. As God dealt with men long ago, so He is dealing with men now also. We now know what God teaches because He spoke through the Prophets and through Jesus.

God did not speak in only one way. He stirred up men in different ways. The Israelites were slaves for 400 years. God chose Moses to go before the king to free his people. God speaks in order that He might set His people free. He spoke not only once but many times. So also today, when we hear the Word of God, we know that God is speaking to us. They are not the words of the speakers, but the words of God.

When Christ had not yet come, the prophets were predicting that He would come. When the time of the prophets passed, Jesus came. Jesus was to come, was to suffer, and was to die. When our Lord did come in the appointed time, He was born of a virgin. He preached the kingdom. But God is no longer using prophets now. He is speaking through His own Son. The same Jesus who made heaven and earth came through Mary to teach and to suffer. God spoke through Him, the appointed one. What He did was perfectly right. Now the Word is here in our hearts. We have here with us the Word of the Gospel. We accept the difficult things of Scripture, for we know that through them God is correcting us.

When Christ had finished suffering for us, He went to heaven. There He is now, interceding for us. There are things that we do not understand, but God teaches us through His Word. God teaches all men. He sent His son in the fullness of time. This is the time for God's Word to be obeyed.

Blood was needed to be shed for us. Christ is the great one who came to do His great work, and is still doing a great work. God finds pleasure in His Son. If we are in Christ, God takes pleasure in us, otherwise not.

Even the angels worship God continually. So also should we. God is satisfied with the work of Christ. So let us also worship the Son. Let our hearts not be indifferent, but take the Word seriously and understand it. We are to give Him praise. The gifts that we have from God are not the same. In our differences let us serve and give God glory.

If we have acknowledged Christ, if we have received His Word, let us set our hearts to it. It is not enough to believe. Trouble weakens us when the Word is not firm in our hearts, but with the Word firm in our hearts we will not be shaken or weakened.

We will bear trouble with assurance. No one can pay for his sin. One can buy his way out of jail, or buy his release, but not so with God. The only way to escape what we rightly deserve from our sins is through Jesus. Let us think of Christ who is our older brother, our Savior. His honor is very great. Let us set our hearts on the Word of God and obey it."

Cross of Decision - To Fight or Not Fight

As the expulsions and threats on their lives escalate, the evangelical Indians of Chiapas face the crucial moral question of whether or not to take up arms to protect themselves. It is not a simple or easy question to answer.

The first genuine theological pacifists were the Buddhists, whose founder demanded from his followers absolute the abstention from any act of violence against their fellow creatures. The Pacific segment of World War II, and the massacres in Cambodia destroyed that great ideal.

In the 3rd Century B.C., India's great king Asoka denounced all forms of war and violence. It helped that he ruled over a secure and well established empire, without barbarians at his borders. Today, journalists sip brandy at the bar of the Asoka hotel in

Delhi, while they wait for the Prime Minister to tell them how many nuclear devices India exploded that day.

In the Western World, pacifism, the bearing of arms for whatever purpose, and war in general became topics for discussion - and division. Some things really never change, the discussions, the divisions, or the wars.

St. Paul wrote to the Romans, "Let every soul be subject to the governing authorities. For there is no authority except from God, and the authors that exist are appointed by God. Therefore whoever resists the authority resists the ordinance of God, and those who resist will bring judgment on themselves. For rulers are not a terror to good works, but to evil. Do you want to be unafraid of the authority? Do what is good, and you will have praise from the same. For he is God's minister to you for good. But if you do evil, be afraid; for he does not bear the sword in vain; for he is God's minister, an avenger to execute wrath on him who practices evil."

St. Augustine believed that limited war was proper as long as it was "just," and "defensive, not offensive." He also believed that all had the "right to protect family and property." Later, he held that a war to resist aggression or to enforce justice might be a Christian duty." His concept of "just" and "unjust" wars is still the official doctrine of the Roman Catholic church.

In the post-reformation period, the Anabaptists, Mennonites and Quakers practiced what they preached: total and complete pacifism. They paid a heavy price for that belief, even when they immigrated to America, but today are still in the forefront of the pacifist movement. Due to political implications, though, they are much less rigid in their practice. After the atomic attack on Hiroshima, people of many denominations became pacifists when they realized what they called the "mutually suicidal character of atomic war."

In Chiapas they are not concerned about atomic weapons. They face AK-47s and machetes. The thinking regarding offensive versus defensive, and self-protection versus taking up arms for self protection, runs the gamut in Chiapas, depending often on who is being attacked by whom.

The Chief Deputy to Bishop Samuel Ruiz, Gonzalo Ituarte, when asked about the Zapatistas in Chiapas and the matter of "just " and "unjust" wars replied, "From the perspective of the Catholic pastoral work. . .we don't agree with the arms struggles, but we understand it clearly, and we understand that it is a 'just' war. We think that the war in Chiapas is not a means to solve the problem, but we still support them, (the Zapatistas) even if they are mistaken."

The general stand of the evangelical church is that, first, we must not get involved in politics and we must evaluate carefully what Jesus meant when He said, "Give to the Emperor what belongs to the Emperor, and give to God what belongs to God," and, "My Kingdom does not belong to this world," and the Apostle Paul's statement, ". . . the existing authorities have been put there by God." Many in the church feel that active resistance will lead to disaster.

Not all agree. There is within the evangelical church a segment that agrees with one son of pacifist missionaries, who has participated is some of the more explosive activities in Chiapas over the past several years. He writes the following in defense of his position:

> Due to the fact that the Chamula brothers have had occasion to defend themselves and their families, and due to the fact that the enemy finds it easy to come in and ruin our witness by casting us out, I find that there is no good answer from our church leadership in relation to what we have done, or should do, in view of attacks against our families and against our brothers. The Government says we have a right to defend ourselves, and that we should do so. I absorbed from childhood the following theology: 'We are pacifists, because Jesus said to turn the other cheek. Furthermore, war is innately evil, it is man's great-

est weapon of destruction and one of the Devil's most powerful tools.' Note that this theology is in line with the 'flower children' of the sixties, who reject war at all costs. In theory this means that we do not let ourselves be kicked out or shut up, but stand and bravely face death. In fact, it has degenerated into cowardice on many cases. A family runs from his community at the first sign of trouble, and asks the Government or the church to then solve his problem. The other extreme case which has happened, and which seems to be twisted in its morality, is the case where evil men come to a Christian's house, walk in and steal what they will, possibly beat the man and his children, rape the wife, and then leave. They are then free to come back and repeat the same in the future. We then say that it was God's will, and we are His willing suffering servants, because He did not defend us, when He could easily have sent an angel to protect us. Thus in the name of God's will we allow uncontested evil; we do not offer any opposition. Is this not a twisted form of justice? Job asked, 'Will not the God of justice do right?' Where did we go wrong? If this is proper and correct, how is it just? If not, why allow it? Are we not responsible to insist on and promote justice in this world?"

Our sister, (Name Withheld) puts the basic question this way, 'What do we do about the bully-boy?' This could also be stated: How do we avoid anarchy if we do not insist on that which is correct, i.e. Justice. We have lived in a 'civilized' society for so long that we are forgetting the issues. We call the police and they take care of the law for us, which is nice. If I say it is wrong to use arms, is it on the grounds that the police will defend me? What happens when there are no police, when the only wall between order and chaos is the church? Do we then ignore the problem? If we do nothing, at the least we will be physically moved aside, which is the case with the 'expulsados,' expelled. The other thing, which has also happened, is that we are tortured and murdered. We need to answer some basic questions in order to establish certain bases."[2]

Charles Malik, former President of the United Nations General Assembly, a man who has been uncompromising in telling world leaders that Jesus Christ is the answer to all the world's problems, has set forth some thoughts on this subject which are worthy of consideration. He writes in his book, Christ and Crisis:

"A Christian thrown into the present world cannot subscribe to any international order just because it affords him a sense of peace and relieves him of the necessity of hard moral decisions. What if the sense of peace were false and illusory? How can he be sure it will not be shattered? What is at stake here is justice, truth, and man. Thus an order that is not based on natural justice, on the dignity of man, and on the trust of truth to vindicate itself, cannot flow from the mind of Christ, nor can it merit His love.

War is terrible, and not only will a Christian not provoke it, but he will do every thing in his power to prevent it from breaking out. But six things do not follow from this: a) it does not follow that if war is forced upon him he will not defend himself; b) nor does it follow that he will not in advance prepare to defend himself, since there is nothing to guarantee that war will not be forced upon him c) nor does it follow that if and when war is forced upon him he will not fight like a man or will not fight for complete victory; d) nor does it follow that, since cold war is a kind of war, he will not fight it to victory; e) nor does it follow that under conditions of war, whether cold or hot, he will blaspheme God and cease to be a Christian, loving Christ above everything else and his neighbor as himself; f) nor, finally, does it follow that, if he is opposed to war, he has any right to be opposed only to that form of war which is 'international,' namely war between the nations, while saying nothing whatsoever about that other form of war which goes by the name of 'class war,' namely war between social and economic classes which could be just as terrible and just as unjust and just as devastating as any so-called 'international war.' It is pride and lack of faith to turn to God and say to Him: 'Look here, I can only live the Christian life under conditions of peace!' What if you are tried precisely under conditions of war! Would you then follow Job's wife's advice and 'curse God, and die' (Job 2:9)? Is it not prudent to prepare even for such a trial? Nothing is more certain from the Christian point of view than that only he who is spiritually prepared to acquit himself honorably under the most trying conditions, including conditions of war, is entitled to enjoy the blessings of peace.

If a Christian faces movements and tendencies that negate Christ and seek to destroy Him, he cannot sit back and do nothing; he must react. He cannot say; it is none of my business, Christ will take care of Himself! Our world is full of such movements and tendencies. Because nothing less than his faith is at stake, the Christian is called upon to witness to his faith perhaps as never before. We really know the grace wherein we stand only when we are pricked in our heart by Christ's tremendous saying: 'Whosoever therefore shall be ashamed of me and of my words in this adulterous and sinful generation; of him also shall the Son of man be ashamed, when he cometh in the glory of his Father with the holy angels' (Mark 8:38; Luke 9:26).

It will be a separate task to work out the many and strange and subtle ways in which this shame expresses itself these days."[3]

Should you use a weapon for protection? This is the crucial

issue facing those who are surrounded by armed men prepared to do evil to them and to their families, and not by judgmental observers sitting safely outside the fray, whose greatest problem is getting a waiter's attention as they sip tea in the Santa Clara Hotel. It is a weighty decision, with potentially serious consequences, that each threatened evangelical must make at the feet of Jesus, seeking His mind on the matter, before the event, not during it.

The Caciques

Another cross the Evangelicals have to bear each day is the domination of the cacique.

Cacique is a Caribbean word that originated during the Aztec reign, a word that is now a painful part of the Mexican vocabulary. After Cortez overthrew Montezuema, and the Aztecs came under Spanish rule, caciques were needed to supervise the slaves who were supplied to the government in lieu of goods. The primary difference in the cacique's new position under the Spanish was that instead of supervising the building of pyramids, they now built churches. As under the Aztecs, they owed their allegiance to a central authority (Spain and Rome), but in practice they worked with considerable autonomy, and were paid handsomely to keep the laborers working.

Today, the cacique gives his allegiance to Mexico City. He is more than a village "chief." He is the principle property owner. Besides owning the land, he controls much of the commerce. This gives him further control over the people of his village, in that most are in debt to him for the basic necessities of life.

The cacique insures his control by maintaining his own army, who are called pistoleros. He is also the person who makes sure that in his village the wishes of Mexico City are carried out at election time, giving the ruling party, the PRI, an uncontested victory, by making sure that all the "agitators" are unavailable to cast their ballots.

The cacique is the one with access to the loudspeaker attached to the top of the local church, announcing important "village meetings," and making sure the church and town retain their "purity," by forcing and coercing "evangelicals" to either give up their faith or leave town.

The cacique maintains his control through traditional fiestas. In this role, it is difficult to separate the cacique from the church, in much the same way that the Aztecs failed to separate the priest's control from that of the Emperor. The two, then as now, are inextricably linked. There are major fiestas for nearly every month of the year, and villages can always find something extra to celebrate: a special saint's day, a birthday, a birth, or a death. The fiesta provides a catharsis for the villagers, not just to come together as one to cement relationships, but also to escape from the drab realities of life. It is expected and acceptable to unlock your inner silence with alcohol and riotous games, letting sentimentality, self-pity and frustrations flow like the supply of posh.

Author Octavio Paz says, "It (the fiesta) is a vital multicolored frenzy that evaporates into smoke, ashes, nothingness. In the aesthetics of perdition, the fiesta is the lodging place of death." Fiestas are an excuse to get drunk, and to openly expresses your feelings of love and hate. Some get loved, others get beaten. All get hurt.

The fiesta typically has four stages:

1. Friends get drunk together.
2. Toasts are made to friendship and past offenses are remembered.
3. The clergy and government are criticized.
4. Extemporaneous and ribald music and songs are played and sung, allowing the participants to express what they would never openly say to anyone while sober.

Not surprisingly, nearly everything needed for the fiesta is commerced through the caciques. Every fiesta, no matter how small or grand, whether it involves one community or many, is by its very nature "religious." It takes place inside and outside the church. Candles must be purchased and burned to please the saints. This is especially true if it is a fiesta honoring one of them. Incense must be bought and burned, so that the "saints" and the gods will enjoy the fiestas with them, and not become angry or jealous if the fiesta is bigger than ones past. Special food must be purchased for the revelers. Religious artifacts have to be placed in homes. Special money gifts are required for the saints, or to whomever the fiesta is dedicated. The most important element of the fiesta, and most expensive, is the "posh," or local beer. Some fiestas go on for several days, even a week, and every day there are candles, offerings, food, and "posh" to buy and consume.

Not supporting the fiesta is an insult to the people of the village, and more importantly, an insult to the saints and the many gods. The elements of celebration cost much more than the average person has to spend. Consequently, the cacique has money to lend, at an average interest rate of 125% per month. After two or three fiestas, a family can sink into debt for the rest of their lives, with each fiesta increasing their indebtedness. It is easy to understand why, when a person becomes an evangelical and refuses to participate in the fiestas, he is a real threat to the cacique's power and position.

When the fiesta is over, there are always those who do not sober up. Alcoholism is a serious problem for Indian men. It increasingly is affecting the women also, as they now are allowed to drink in public. Intoxication is no longer just a part of the fiestas, but of everyday life. The sight of drunk or unconscious Indians is becoming tragically common.

One Indian leader, with anger and frustration, tells anyone who will listen, "With political power given by the government, the caciques prevent our remote villages from being provided with adequate food, health, education and communications, because it is evidently easier to control a hungry, sick and ignorant people."

It is a 500 year old system that has made many a man and organization rich and powerful. Little wonder that those in power have done nothing to change it.

The Zapatistas (EZLN)

The protracted Chiapan rebellion is a burden for both the body of Christ and every individual Indian there. It has a way of making everyone its prisoner. It is no longer enough to attempt to remain neutral. Indians are now being confronted with the question: whose side are you on? An incorrect answer to this question can have dire consequences.

The Zapatistas stand out in the villages, with their uniform of dark brown shirts, charcoal pants and sturdy hiking boots. Few wear masks now, since the drama has worn off. Nevertheless, their presence is intimidating to non-sympathizers.

Mexico City has begun to execute a general strategy for attacking the rebellion, in which they move into one town at a time, neutralizing the Zapatistas and keeping them under control by permanently stationing soldiers in the town. Civil rights groups call this action a military occupation and suppression.

This means that the average Indian is having to live with the daily threat of deadly conflict, like the one that took place late in the evening of June 11, 1998.

Lookouts had warned the village that government troops were positioned on the outskirts of town. Most of the villagers had run to their shacks, lying on the floor with their children, a weapon by their side, if they had one. The Zapatistas took rehearsed positions, but the government soldiers soon forced them to flee. In less than a day of fighting, the soldiers moved on, except for those now permanently stationed in town to guard against the Zapatista's return. Nine dead and twice as many wounded were the human toll of the rebellion that day.

When the villagers cautiously came out of their shacks and saw the strewn bodies, they realized that this had only been a dress rehearsal for what was inevitably yet to come. The swaggering young men and kids that made up the Zapatistas had disappeared into the jungle, leaving behind a banner with the following message for the government troops: "For each of the sympathizers killed in this battle, we will kill 10 government soldiers." But everyone knew their departure would be short-lived. They would return in civilian clothes and attempt to recruit and rebuild their force.

The tragedy is that the people of both armies say they are attempting to help the Indians, who, with enough affliction already, are the real victims in the end. Fighting the soil, wresting one more stalk of corn from the ground, doing daily battle with disease and malnutrition, and dealing with a life of poverty is battle enough for anyone.

―――――― ✳ ――――――

On Monday morning, the sun rose to greet the girls. Together, they knelt by the single bed and spoke with their Creator. Beyond them, the rest of the village awoke. Some went to the fields, some to bottle, some to the church to light candles and beseech the mercy of the spirits. Beyond their imagination, rebels schemed, the wealthy dreamed, and an unseen battle raged. But here in this corner, there was no interruption as three young girls knelt before the highest power in heaven.

On Tuesday morning, Rosa brought her children. With two more little ones, the walls of the hut protested the crowd that pushed and shoved the empty space and left too little to spare. But the chaos didn't divert them, and the three young warriors came again before Jehovah. Tuesday turned to Wednesday, and Wednesday spilled into Thursday. But while the five children worked and played, they did not forget the threat, and faithfully acknowledged their faith in Creator God's control.

When Friday came, they woke as every other morning. In the distance, the tinkle of fiesta preparations began. The villagers rested from their work in the fields, and scurried about hanging streamers, gathering flowers, spreading straw on the square and feeding their choicest chickens a final meal. Women wove beautiful yarns into their hair, and the men donned their traditional white woolen sweaters. Even the littlest children sensed the excitement, and raced about the paths of the village. Vendors set up an array of sacred items which would be necessary for the fiesta: costly candles, images, and shining rows of posh in bottles.

Behind the trees on the edge of town, three young sisters and their cousins began preparations of their own. Pasquala brought a pail from the well, and they scrubbed their faces in the cold water. The table in the center of the hut remained empty and untended. Today, while the town gorged themselves on food an drink in the presence of the god of the underworld, this house would remain focused in prayer to another God.

Pasquala, her confidence restored, led their vigil. Today they would work at her favorite chore: flower gathering. Tourists in San Cristobal loved to buy flowers. Maybe it was just the romantic image of the flower vendor. The brown earth tones of native skin contrasted with the flower's bright light. The bowed back of a flower seller, weighted by the load of nature's beauty, was an irony too easily noticed, and quickly forgotten. No matter. Pasquala loved to gather flowers and sell them to the careless tourists.

The hidden gardens of mountain wild flowers proved a marvelous place to escape this Friday. Here the fingerprints of some eternal artist hollowed a cradle for those who would notice it. Pasquala and her charges romped about the colorful slopes and flower beds. Each girl wrapped a blanket about their back and filled the homemade pouch with bushels of bright petals. Nothing in the sky spoke of impending danger, not a single cloud. They ripped at the grass as they ran through it, flinging it into the air above them. Their laughter was their song of praise, lifting it high above them to the delight of the Maker.

The sun passed its peak, and the pendulum of day began swung towards dusk. Pasquala called the children, and together they collected their sweetly scented treasures, hoisting them onto their backs for the hike home. They reached the door of their hut still filled with the joy of today's celebration. Yet hunger returned with them, nipping at their bellies. For a while, though, they sat in the doorway, relishing the final conflict between sun and starlight.

Pasquala stretched her legs before her, and feeling the clean fatigue that follows children's play. She leaned against the wood slat walls, and took her niece onto her skirted lap. Cries and chaotic sounds from the fiesta sifted through the trees in a broken crescendo, but did not disturb the peace of those in Pasquala's house. The looming finger of aunt Marta's dire words held little power over them, for they were satisfied to rest in the presence of God.

The day long fast united them in purpose. Pasquala began to pray. "Jevovah-Jesus." She was speaking to God. Her voice was free from any religious piety. Catch phrases, careless approaches to God, plastic humility, and strained eloquence were absent. She approached the Master with pure sincerity.

"Jehovah-Jesus." The rest cannot be recorded. Perhaps it never came in words audible to the human ear, blemished by mortal interpretation. No words were needed. The purity of children's prayer is a marvel of the Creator, allowing a human creation the ability to communicate with its Creator. So it was that young Pasquala prayed, emptying her heart of fear, overflowing with the day's happiness, looking into eyes she couldn't physically see. Peace covered her, and a song filled her breast, spilling over her lips:

"There is no God as big as You . . .

There is no God that can do the works like those that you do . . ."

Beneath the iris of the moon, the children joined their orphaned guardian with whispered voices. As they crawled backwards into the shelter of their hut and closed the door behind them, the song still trickled through their mind.

"There is no God as big as You."

Pasquala tucked her nieces into a blanket on the dirt floor, just beneath the overhang of the single sagging bed. Here they felt safe, resting in the shadow of Pasquala's bed, hidden from the dangers of the night. In the bed, Pasquala huddled close to her sisters. Just like their mother taught them in her lifetime, they balled up their shirts and used them for pillows. Their thick wool skirts served as blankets, and between their three bodies there was enough heat to ward off the night's cold advances.

The stars anchored the sails of the midnight sky, and all was calm.

Pasquala slept. Like an infant in the security of a mother's breast, she slipped away from reality and drifted into a world of dreams. In the haze of her unconsciousness, she floated through a pool of hazy colors and images. No real plot developed, only the gentle ebb and flow of pictures. It was warm here beyond the reach of night and hunger pangs.

Then a sound scraped the blurry surface of her dream. In the warm river of her imagination she felt a sudden chill. There again. A snarl. A low rumble coming from deep within some animal, forewarning an attack. Pasquala shuddered in her dream and looked about the peaceful sea of color that was quickly turning stormy. The snarl came again, insistent of attention. She could not see the animal from which it came, but could feel the hair that lined its neck begin to rise in tense preparation. From behind bared teeth and curled lip, she felt the wide-eyed heat of the animal's fear, as its growl erupted in a bark that pitched her into consciousness. She jumped awake.

All was dark within the hut. The sounds of the fiesta slurred into silence, and her two sisters lay fast asleep beside her. Her chest trembled with her racing heartbeat, and she struggled to fight out of the dream. The straw roof above her stared down complacently; she could see a crack of starlight through a tiny hole in its cover. The dog barked again. Now she was awake.

Their dog was only one of a plethora of mixed breed scavengers that roamed the streets of every town in Mexico who had adopted them as his own. Each day he stole a corner in the shade beneath their roof, and chased any mice unfortunate enough to encroach upon their little home. Tonight Pasquala had tied him to a stick just outside her hut to keep him from disappearing on his nightly escapades. While she had fallen into bed without an anxious thought, she always appreciated Perro's company, even if it was unwilling.

She rolled out of bed, careful not to step on her nieces, who were curled up on the floor beneath her. Perro must be hungry. She had unthinkingly included him in their fast today, and a dog's devotion rarely requires an endurance of hunger. Groping through the darkness, Pasquala hunted for something for him to eat. His barks continued to cut the silence, urgently pleading for attention, approaching an hysterical pitch.

Still somewhat stupefied with sleep, Pasquala stumbled to the door to calm the dog. The stupid creature would wake her sisters if he continued any longer. She took one footstep out the door, and then she saw it. Her stomach crashed into her chest, and fear struck like a serpent. In the shadowed darkness, a blackened figure with lantern stumbled out of sight behind the corner of her hut. For a frozen instant, she tried to comprehend the meaning of this firebearing phantom, but could not move her mouth to scream.

A scent of sweetness filtered through her paralyzed mind, and cried the warning: "Gasoline!" Then hell broke free from beneath the earth, and sprayed a geyser of flame over the back corner of Pasquala's home. Perro recovered the wild in his blood and broke the rope that bound him to the scene. His howls followed him into the distance, and shattered the spell of fear that held Pasquala paralyzed. She wasn't dreaming. Spinning towards the doorway, she let a shriek escape: "Sisters!"

She must free them from coiling flames that were eating their tinder hut alive. The wild glow lit the profile of her face in eerie luminosity, framing her frightened figure in flame. But as the child mother leaped to save her babies, another phantom shadow crawled from the nightmare to her doorstep. She only saw him for an instant, among the blurred images of the inferno behind the house, the open doorway, and her sleeping sisters. He stepped between her and the door, his woolen vest and white sombrero betraying his humanity. This was not a phantom, this was a man.

"Who has come to kill me?" screamed the girl into the terror of her mind.

The man stepped towards her and confirmed his purpose. In his hands he held a stick of metal that exploded when he pushed it towards her. Pasquala's bare shoulder boiled with heat. Scalding pain seared her skin like kettle water. Above the smell of gasoline and gunpowder, she tasted the scent of her own blood. The man moved to fire upon the child again, and the adrenaline boiled inside her as she turned and ran.

As terror drives startled deer to wide-eyed flight, so Pasquala's legs obeyed lightning charges from her brain and carried her away. Without aim or logic, she ran to escape this man who chased her with his gun. Rocks in the ground tore at her bare feet and branches ripped her bare skin. She heard the man panting behind her, but nimble youth and fear of death kept her out of his reach. Blood ran into her left eye, and her neck and shoulder filled with pain. Her flight took her towards the field, but the phantoms multiplied in the darkness.

Another man stepped out to block her path. My God, how many have come here to kill me? This one was too close, and she could not avoid him. She could not see his face, nor did she wish to. What expression etches the face of a man whose prey is little children? His arms lurched out to her, to close this disgraceful chapter of an orphan girl's unfaithfulness. Then Pasquala saw the hole. As if the hands of God had opened up a pathway through these waters of death, she saw a gap to freedom. She shifted only slightly, and slipped just beyond his clutches. The angry man's fingers slapped on her left arm, straining to snatch her back, but the torn and bloody surface of her skin merely slipped through his claws, and Pasquala was away.

Their angry calls dimmed behind her and her heaving breath filled the gathering silence. Furrowed ground beneath her feet identified the cornfield she had entered. Her trembling stride faltered over a hole in the dirt, and she stumbled to her knees. The adrenaline was tapering off, and the fasting of yesterday magnified her weakening condition. Her mind was deep in shock, and the distant glow of her burning hut hardly registered upon her emotions. In self defense, her mind closed its doors to stimulus. Besides a hazy realization that her sisters must be dead, she didn't feel much more than thirst. Incredible thirst. Her mouth was caked with dried saliva that crusted at the edges of her lips.

She must have a drink. The well could not be far. She crawled along the sunbaked soil, still hard and dry by the light of the moon. Time must have passed, but she had no sense of it. Placing one knee in front of the other and dragging her mangled arm beside her, she crawled until she felt the cool rock rim of the well. A sheep or two loitered nearby, sleepily awaiting the morning. They stared at her unblinkingly, oblivious to her pain. Ladling some water into her mouth, she winced as it revived her senses and her pain.

Water's cool refreshment brought a twinge of agonized lucidity. "All this they did because of the Creator God," was the thought that came into her mind, though she could not grasp nor understand it. Tears came, not in the cleansing weeping of sadness, but only in a stunned reaction to this nightmare's undeniable reality.

The blood on her neck and arm and shoulder began to dry, crusting the wounds, which cracked open again at the slightest movement. Metal shrapnel had pierced her skin and settled deep below its surface. Blood loss made her dizzy, and she lay beside the well collecting her strength. She could not stay here long. The men would find her, finishing this sacrifice they intended. Her body began to shake with shock, and chills chased up and down her limbs. In a mighty effort, Pasquala battled to balance on her feet again, then wobbled along the edge of the field towards the safety of the trees.

She needed help. Although a strong girl for thirteen years of age, Pasquala was badly injured, and entirely exhausted. There was little hope of getting help from any of the neighbors. After all, any one of them could have been among the phantoms who haunted her home this evening. Even so, with the fiesta just completed, most of them were probably filled with the effects of the sacred alcohol and the thought of approaching another inebriate made her ankles tremble violently. The only face that came to mind without a knife of dread was that of Agustino. As she moved her body mechanically through the woodlands, she remembered the day Agustino introduced them to Jehovah-God. Despite the limits of her memory, she could still recall the blur of happiness that came the day Gustavo was healed. It was all so far away.

Along the ragged path she pushed herself, relying on instinct to carry her to Agustino's doorstep. Death whispered behind her, in the the rustle of the wings that once filled her mind with horrible dreams in the days before she met the God who took her fear away. Now that fear was back, chasing her from her burning hut, hounding her through the furrowed fields, and nipping at her heels along this mountain trail. She realized she wasn't going to make it. She didn't really want to make it, after all. Death seemed so much easier than the agony of living through this moment. But onward she limped, unable to simply lie down and allow the darkness to swallow her.

Minutes passed, hours passed, years passed, until finally, she fell at Agustino's doorstep. Much in the same posture as her sister Rosa had fallen at his doorway many months before, Pasquala pitched against the wooden door with all the momentum her broken frame could muster.

"Agustino."

Silence. The trees around her lay still. Crickets called back and forth across the woods along Agustino's cornfield, singing their ancient song in cheerful ignorance to the tragedy unraveling in their midst. But all the rest was still, still as death.

"My God, help me." Pasquala sobbed and beat the wooden door again. Enough pain churned within her to make anger, and anger gave her strength.

"Agustino!" She called louder. "Agustino!"

For a moment silence prevailed, and her head dropped in hopelessness. Then a rustle came from within the ex-healer's house. Muttering and grumbling through the unlit hut, Agustino cracked the door. He squinted in agitation.

"Why do you come in the night?" It was the way of Agustino.

Then his vision cleared, and he saw the horrible scene before him. Her eyes caught him first, this young girl, terror filling the dark pool of her eyes, upturned and pleading for relief. One ashamed hand tried to shield her body, while the other hung limp from the end of a mangled arm. The left side of her torso was wet with oozing, cracked blood. Child-soft skin on her neck and shoulder hung in shreds, raked by claws of steel. It was Pasquala.

"My child!" he gasped, gathering her carefully in his arms and drawing her inside.

"Agustino." It was all she could manage through the tide of feeling that swept her battered body. All the independence of this child, who had stood so strong every moment of her life, now dissolved in the arms of someone who made her feel safe. The words came out in gasps and sobs and a jumble of nonsense that crushed Agustino's heart to hear.

"They. . . burned our house. . . fire. . . killed . . . sisters. . . gun. . . fiesta. . . because . . . Creator God."

Agustino understood enough. He too, had heard the threats, and the tumult of growing dissension in the village. He feared such an attack on his own house, but never imagined they would wage their battle on mere children. But the cowards had. It was madness. And now this girl needed his help. As for the others, they were probably already dead. He spoke gently to the girl clinging to him. "We must get you to San Cristobal."

His wife was now wide awake, and rushed around their dwelling, gathering clothing for the child. She wrestled back the tears that threatened to erupt from within her, knowing she must remain composed, if only for the sake of the poor, panicked girl who was now curled up in the fetal position on their floor, sucking her thumb.

The preparations buzzed around her, but Pasquala had little concept of what transpired. She was glad to let someone else handle the responsibility this one time in her life. Agustino held a cup of water to her lips, and she tried to sip it without choking. Finally, he stood up.

"I will carry you, child." It was a genuine offer. Despite the years that crooked his back and left him lying in bed far too often these days, Agustino meant to carry her on his back.

Pasquala climbed gingerly to her feet. Agustino and his wife spun in circles around her.

"No, I can walk." She knew he could not carry her. Besides, all the pain that brewed within her would not let her rest on someone else's back. So they set out for San Cristobal. It was the middle of the night, but high above them, the moon shown down and offered a hint of guiding light. This lesser of the lights was the sad witness of the eternity of evil that had played out beneath its glow.

Pasquala hobbled slowly up the road. Drops of red broke free from her crusted shoulder and fell onto the dusty road. The thirstily soil drank each drop, erasing any trace of their passage. Once, Agustino stopped and simply said, "Let's pray to the Creator God, because He is so big." Pasquala complied, although she was numb, and she had no strength to think. With that, the man continued shuffling along beside her, but in the quiet of his head he stayed before the Big God.

Step. Step. Step. The road stretched before them, climbing hills and skirting trees, plunging down along the valley's edge and creeping ever closer to the city of San Cristobal. The moon dropped lower in the sky, ashamed of the evil its light revealed, bowing to the greater sun. Stars slipped behind the curtain of gathering daylight, and behind and above them skies burned with the pure fire of dawn. Time lost all meaning to these two pilgrims. When at last they reached the entrance to the square of San Cristobal, the bells in the steeple of the Cathedral clanged eight times in mocking welcome.

White dresses, white floors, white walls, white eyes, white-washed expressions . . . everything in the hospital was sterile white. Devoid of color, devoid of texture, devoid of any character of dirt, the blinding coldness of this place matched the condition of her soul. Agustino held her shivering hand in his, and helped her climb onto the silver table top. She looked for her reflection, but saw only the sparkling whiteness of the ceiling tiles. A doctor dressed in blue explained to her in a broken form of the Tzotzil dialect what he was going to do.

She had never been behind the walls of a hospital, and had her mind not been dead with shock would have offered a more violent protest. In her own tradition, doctors were enemies and not to be trusted. They wielded small sharp knives, and offered strange white pellets that would disappear in water. Some said these pellets made headaches disappear, but most knew that this was only a compelling magic that would anger the spirits and displace their own healers.

As the doctor spoke to Pasquala, she drifted in and out of consciousness. Her feet were numb and bloody from the terrible pilgrimage from the village. The doctor's lips were moving; she heard his voice, then it disappeared again, while his lips continued to move. How strange this was. Then through the confusion of the doctor's voice and mismatched lips, she saw a woman enter in clothing like the doctor's. She held a silver pail of water and some pieces of coarse cloth. The pail of water bubbled with foam. The woman dipped her cloth into the pail and moved closer to Pasquala. She heard the doctor's voice fading in and out, ". . . must clean. . . wound . . . infection . . . swelling . . ." The rest was lost.

What followed was agony. The woman took the cloth and placed it on Pasquala's bloody arm. Excruciating pain leaped up her neck and sliced like razors in her head. A face as gentle as the woman's in the paper gown was a cruel disguise for behavior so unkind. Pasquala unearthed the pathetic cry of a coyote pup stuck in a hunter's trap. Scraping along the surface of Pasquala's arm, the doctor's assistant tore off dried blood and jagged skin, leaving fire as hot as the shotgun blast which had torn into her flesh.

Thus the wound was purified, and through the anguished yelps of her protest, which had subsided into despairing sobs, Agustino kept his hand upon her head and tried to comfort her. "Don't cry daughter, they are here to heal you." He sounded almost unconvinced himself, as Pasquala's cries cut into his own heart, hurting with greater pain than if the hurt were his to bear. The doctor brought a white towel, wrapping it about the wound to soak up the blood that now flowed with renewed energy. In simple terms, he explained to Agustino that removing all the shotgun pellets would be a job far too complicated and painful, and that if they simply left them where they lay, the skin would heal back over them. Eventually, only the scars would remain. But now, the girl desperately needed rest and nourishment.

Pasquala finally succumbed to the pull of unconsciousness. But while her eyes were darkening, her ears still caught flickering conversations. A stranger's voice mumbled somewhere, and she heard Agustino's voice responding a grave tone.

". . . her sisters both are dead. One burned in the fire . . . all that's left are a skull and piece of bone . . . yes the other died as well . . . no, not in the fire . . . machete slash across the neck . . . terrible . . . huddled by two others . . . yes both remained alive . . . one cut badly in the face and arm . . . brought her in an hour ago . . . may lose the arm . . . poor child is still unconscious . . . may not know until its gone . . . other child . . . yes the smallest girl . . . cut her too, across the arms and slashed about the neck . . . tried to save her . . . carried half way here to San Cristobal . . . never made a sound . . . finally she ceased to breathe . . . we took her back to bury her . . . beautiful little girl . . ."

Somewhere within her own delirium, Pasquala sorted through the cuttings of conversation. She never really heard the words over the screams of her sisters, furrowed by the rusty edge of the machete. Screams from the flames that twisted round about a writhing body, leaving none but smoke and smoldering embers. Screaming cries to their Great God, whose healing hand could not be seen. The screaming of her own voice, reaching for the surface of the conscious world. This sound woke her from the nightmares, and she begged for all to be a dream. One glance at Agustino's weeping form, bent prostrate on the floor, confirmed the vision's reality.

This time she did not struggle, letting the broken limits of her mind cast her into a coma's refuge. All that day she slept, then through the night, then on into another day. At times she felt her body climbing back for air, but she dragged it down again, in stubborn refusal to face the world that stood poised to strike her. There was safety here behind the walls of sleep, where the future could move forward without her participation.

Agustino sat beside her bed and held her hand, watching the closed eyelids defiantly barricade the doorway to the soul beneath. From time to time a tear slipped through the seal, a message from the world behind her silence, and Agustino knew that time would bring her back. Rosa joined him at the bedside. She too had little left to say. One daughter was dead. She died in someone else's arms, someone who could not carry her to San Cristobal fast enough. They said she asked for her mommy, through dried-up lips and blood-caked eyes. Rosa did not even get to say good-bye, because the villagers had buried the child's remains before Rosa returned from the coast. Her aunt Marta was there to see the passing on, and told her carelessly that there was really nothing left to see.

Rosa's other daughter lay in a bed not far from Pasquala's. Her arm was almost severed by the machete, and the doctors didn't know if they could save it. She was only seven. Without an arm, she would never find a husband, never weave a basket, never thread a bracelet. Before her life had yet begun, she was destined for a street corner with a plastic cup and pitiful face, cast upon the mercy of some sympathetic tourist who flipped her a coin or two. Rosa wept again.

After several days, Pasquala could stay underneath the blanket of oblivion no longer, and she opened her eyes onto the barren whiteness of the hospital room again. At first she could see nothing more than cold, bright, artificial light. Then something else slipped into blurry focus, something moving, something living, something crying. It was Rosa. Pasquala tried to call her sister's name, but her mouth was thick and uncooperative. More whiteness covered her shoulder, wound around her neck, and bound her arm against her body. It was soft and clean, though marked with spots of leaking blood.

Rosa jumped to kiss her, and tried to wrap her arms around the clumsy envelope of gauze that held Pasquala helpless. The tears that dripped upon her face were cool, and made Pasquala awkward. She had rarely seen her sister cry, it was not the custom of their people. Then the images from her unconsciousness came back, and she knew the awful truth would never be reversed. Her sisters were dead, and she would never sing a song with them again.

Agustino joined the wavering frame of vision, and stroked her hair with his wrinkled hand. How kind he was, and so gentle. "Don't cry my child," he began with moisture in his own eyes. "They are with Jehovah-Jesus now."

The words were soft and sincere, but Pasquala felt the

barbs of deep betrayal pulling anger to her eyes.

"I can't believe," was all she said. Jehovah-Jesus left her
sisters in the fire. Jehovah-Jesus let children die. Jehovah-
Jesus let their tender hearts believe that He would stay beside
them, and where was he when death came creeping through the
night? Sure, he chased the dreams away. Sure he quelled their
fears. Or was that something else? Was it just a trick?
Perhaps the wonderful fantasy of a God who had power over all
other gods was nothing more than wild fables and magic stories from a distant land.

"I can't believe," came the moan from the furthest corner
of her broken heart. Upon her chest a mountain of sadness set
its whole weight. It wrung her breath and crushed her will in its
mighty jaws, and she could not find the strength to fight. If
only sadness were a wild beast, whose neck she could take
between her child's hands and break with all the savage anger
that sprung from her. If she could feel its teeth upon her skin
rather than her soul, she would happily allow it. The throbbing
ache beneath the bandage cold not compare to what fed upon
the carcass left inside her. It ate away beyond her reach, and
drug her down into its lair.

She needed to vomit, but there was nothing in her stomach. She wanted to scream but didn't have the energy. She
wanted out of this cage, but the bandages bound her. She
wanted her sisters back. She wanted to die. So she cried. In
the morning, tears awoke her. In the night, tears washed her
into sleep. Agustino wondered that the colored richness in her
eyes didn't muddy in the flow. Day after day he or his wife would
sit by her bed and speak to the Creator God he still believed in,
begging restoration on her behalf.

He didn't understand it, this simple farmer who once used
the darkness for a certain healing magic. He didn't know why
God above all gods would let the spirits take the lives of these
beloved children. Agustino could not answer Pasquala's doubt
and disbelief. She was but a child herself, and who could mend

the heart of a child? But he refused to not believe. He still would clench her hand and carry her to the throne of heaven. There he offered her before the Maker God, and asked for the Healer's caress to mend this bruised little reed.

Days stretched into weeks. Pasquala's body mended slowly, but her spirit lay in tired surrender. Her eyes, deflated of all youth's vision, mirrored the flatness of hospital white. She felt a comfort in Agustino's presence, and when he prayed aloud a twinge of light stirred through her hopelessness. But he could not bring back her sister's happy chatter, and in a sense, he made her angry for his conviction in a God that apparently did not exist.

One afternoon as she lay in her bed, tears dried and face blank, a tiny window allowed a beam of true, pure light into the room. Tired of the monotonous depression that bound her in the waking hours, she drifted off to sleep's escape. The spotless walls and gleaming surfaces tipped and fell into a quiet fog, and her eyes turned inward seeking peace. For some moments she was numb, unthinking and unaware. Sleep was a drug, bought for the price of time, and often the thinker's singular relief.

But in her sweet retreat, a whisper interrupted.

"Pasquala."

Her heartbeat hesitated. The voice was distant but familiar. Again it came. "Pasquala." Louder. Insistent. Closer. She opened her eyes. The room still stood around her in naked white, still and empty. The curtains on the tiny window rustled in a sunlit breeze, but silence was the only sound. She strained her ears, and searched for the strange hallucination.

"Pasquala!" The voice came in her ear this time, loud and undeniable. It was. It couldn't be. It was. From beyond the reach of death, beyond the suffocation of the fire-eaten house, beyond the slashes of machetes came her sister's voice. It wasn't possible. What cruel trick did death play on her now?

Pasquala wept again, salty, bitter sadness washing her shallow cheeks. Even sleep was no escape.

"Pasquala . . . why do you cry?" It was her other sister, speaking to her from some place unseen. The voice was curious, even perplexed. As if she didn't know! Pasquala wanted to strike out, to face this spirit who dared to taunt her in her dreams. Was this a dream? The room was here, cold and bare, curtains tickling in the window frame. Then she felt the touch. A hand upon her shoulder, soft and tender, a child's cautious caress. Through the bandage on her other side, she felt a different hand. Pasquala felt no fear, no startled surprise, no urge to flee from this invisible comforter. But the tears came faster now, and she knew who stood beside her.

"Why are you here?" she choked from underneath the mountain in her chest. "They killed you both . . . " Her voice trickled off into unspeakable grief.

"We're not dead," her sisters giggled with delight. "We're alive, and living here with God!" Pasquala felt them tilt their heads to see each other laugh, so amused with this silly game of theirs. She felt the mountain move and fall into some eternal sea, where mountains have no strength, tears can drown, and sorrow dies. Gasping in the darkness hanging in her soul, the final ember of her smoldering wick sucked in the air of freedom. Sputtering like dampened tinder, it fought for life beneath the tender breath that swirled from the Healer's lungs. Fragile in the wind of her confusion, the spark glowed hot then faded orange. But that gentle breath that moved to fill her touched the dying fire and coaxed it into flame.

She tried to turn and see the girls, but her bandages restricted her and they remained just out of sight. Fumbling with the words, she strained to speak. "What is it like there with God? Are there many people?"

"Oh yes," they assured her, struggling not to laugh again. "There are many people here, and many houses too!"

Pasquala wanted to join them. She longed to be there with them, to share a house again. She wanted to laugh with them, and leave these bandages here in the white cotton bed. She wanted to meet the Creator God who lived there with them. Questions spun about her brain in a dizzying circus of euphoria.

And then the hands lifted from her shoulder. The laughter danced off far away and the silence resonated with the echo. She opened her eyes.

The room still lay before her, white and cold and painful in its reality. Agustino stood beside her, hardly able to stand still, so great was the joy that filled his limbs. He could see it in her eyes. She knew! He wanted to shout, to sing, to beat the drum, he wanted to cry.

"Agustino, they're alive with God." Pasquala murmured in amazement, the fire now burning in her breast. Again the water filled her eyes, but this time it bubbled and gurgled across her face, filling the cracks that laughter made. She knew.

Beyond the tiny window where the curtains danced, darkness cast its shroud on day and snuffed the fire of the sun. Beneath the gravity of night, a cross of candles drowned in waxen puddles and froze atop a mother's grave. Beyond the quiet village where a child's home once stood, the ashes cooled and scattered in a restless wind.

But in this child of the Greatest God, fear fled the light and the fire of freedom blazed.

IN CONCLUSION

Thus says the Lord God: "Behold, I am against the shepherds . . . I
shall deliver My flock from their mouth, that they may not be food
for them . . . Behold, I Myself will search for My sheep and seek
them out . . . I will seek the lost, bring back the scattered, bind up
the broken, and strengthen the sick . . Behold I, even I, will judge
between the fat sheep and the lean sheep, because you push . . .and
thrust at all the weak with your horns . . . I will judge between one
sheep and another. As for you, My sheep, the sheep of My pasture,
You are men, and I am your God.

Ezekiel 34:10-11,16,20-22,31

As was stated at the beginning of this book, the history of Chiapas is the story of a people who are driven by an inborn understanding of the supernatural power of blood. Tragically, it has been the native people themselves who have forever been the source of the country's sacrificial offerings. Mayan priests first demanded their blood to appease the gods of the sun, the moon, and the rain. Five centuries ago, the Spanish conquistadors, driven by their gods of silver and gold, offered up millions of native lives on the altars of uncontrolled greed.

Today, the lives of native Chiapans continue to be sacrificed by a nation that is hungry for power, prosperity, and acceptance into the global market. They are the victims of bullying and extortion by their local village bosses, their land has been stolen from them by the powerful mestizo government which has broken a century of promises in failing to return it, and they have been kept powerless and ignorant by a church which has spiritually blinded them with the half truths of syncretism.

The danger today is that the western world, occupied with its own problems, looks at Chiapas and says, "Heal thyself." "You have had your fifteen minutes of television fame," we say. "Now we are interested in something else." In so doing, powerlessness has left the Indians with no choice but to turn to the sword of rebellion, encouraged by the priest's deceptive theology of liberation. Instead of gaining freedom, the Indians have again been sacrificed by their political leaders. The theology of liberation, which comes so close to touching both the heart of Jesus and the Indian's heart as well, has failed to accomplished its purpose, because it ignores the gift of the Healer's blood. Only this lacking element can truly bring them "peace that passes all understanding."

It is difficult, if not impossible, for an outside observer to truly understand the difficulties and frustrations of the native Chiapans. However, a long time Chiapan missionary, who with her husband has spent most of her adult life in Chiapas, is qualified to give an analysis of the situation. She writes: "As you know, there are many voices crying in the wilderness of misinformation.

Take a mixture of geological distance, sociological separation, monolingualism, tribal independence and traditions, religious and party fanaticism, government fear and ineptitude, the drive for money by any means, drugs, Indian cacique pressures, easy acquisition of arms for mentally ignorant power groups, and add to that the world's present 'humane' penchant for daily dramatic news bites which decry government and army, and you end up inevitably with something like the present chaos we are experiencing in some parts of Chiapas."

Liberation Theology

In discussing Chiapas, you cannot ignore Liberation Theology. Lost in all the left-of-center literature today are several important unasked and unanswered questions:

1. Does Liberation Theology value spiritual re-birth, spiritual riches and eternal life? Or is it interested only in the here-and-now, fighting anyone who disagrees?

2. In the Beatitudes, Christ uses the term "blessed" to mean "happy." Does getting plenty to eat and drink and a comfortable place to live really make a person "blessed?" If so, why aren't all rich people happy?"

3. Does not Liberation Theology place an inordinate emphasis on the material aspects of life?

4. Does not Liberation Theology's sole concern for the "poor" relegate the rest of God's Word to a level of unimportance?

Liberation Theology proclaims that "God is on the side of the oppressed." While this is true, isn't He also on the side of the oppressor? Don't both need the saving grace of our Lord Jesus Christ, which is missing in this truncated gospel?

During the U.S. Civil War, one of Lincoln's generals told Lincoln, "We will win (this war) because God is on our side."

Lincoln replied, "That is not my worry. My worry is whether or not we are on God's side."

No less wise are the words of two true revolutionaries. Archbishop Oscar Romero wrote, "It would be worthless to have an economic liberation in which all the poor had their own house, their own money, but were all sinners, their hearts estranged from God. What good would it be? There are nations at present that are economically and socially quite advanced, for example those of northern Europe, and yet how much vice and excess!

"The church will always have it word to say: conversion. Progress will not be completed even if we organize ideally the economy and the political and social orders of our people. It won't be entire with that. That will be the basis, so that it can be completed by what the church pursues and proclaims: God adored by all, Christ acknowledged as only Savior, deep joy of spirit in being at peace with God and with our brothers and sisters.

Let us not put our trust in earthly liberation movements. Yes, they are providential, but only if they do not forget that all the liberating force in the world comes from Christ."

The second revolutionary, who put himself directly in harm's way, giving his life for his revolution, was Martin Luther King Jr. who said, "True greatness is not where one stands in comfort and confidence, but where one stands in conflict."

So, the question being for the people of Chiapas, Mexico is, "who do you wish to follow, a rebel or a revolutionary?

The Zapatistas (EZLN)

The Zapatistas are rebels who think of themselves as reformers. No one doubts that Marcos, Ruiz and others, in the deepest part of their being, want to see the Indians treated with dignity, instead of being humiliated, beaten and repressed. The problem is that after the uprising in San Cristobal in 1994, and the media frenzy that followed, they began to believe their own press. The

Zapatistas are not only not revolutionary, they don't fit the definition of an armed movement. They have more followers than weapons. Skirmishes with the Mexican Army are few and far between, unless the Army initiates the conflict. Not moving beyond their strongholds, which are often occupied by Indians who want to leave and get on with their own lives, the Zapatista's survival depends on the protective mantle of national and world public opinion, but the spotlight has diminished from live CNN coverage to an occasional sound byte. As one historian puts it, "The Zapatista Army is not a Mexican version of the heroic guerrillas of the Sierra Maetra. Its members may be heroic, but they are not guerrillas."[1]

The danger is that Mexico City may ignore the true issues brought by the Indians, and instead build them a cultural hall or cathedral in San Cristobal, or take some of the land cases that have been hidden in the courts for a decade or more, promising to review them, but ultimately never reaching a decision.

A second danger is that the EZLN, only one of thirty-seven armed insurgence groups in Chiapas, may merge with the much more disciplined Revolutionary's Popular Army (EPR), who have told the nation, "we are starting an armed struggle against antipopular government, which defends foreign interests and big business." Ironically, foreign monies, armies, and sympathy are accepted by this group.

As seen in Mexico's history, when the economy is good, the stock market is up, and the price of coffee doubles, the "good life" never reaches down to the Indians, who provide the foundation of the economy by producing much of what is sold. In a fifty billion dollar governmental bailout, they were the last to receive help. As Andres Oppenheimer reports in his book, Bordering On Chaos, Mexico is not "facing a classic people's revolution, but a gradual meltdown."

The sad aspect is that, in the end, the Indians are no better off, and are perhaps worse off, than they were when the rebellion started. It is going to take more than a political victory for either side to win.

Sub-Comandante Marcos

You cannot separate the Zapatistas from their self-anointed leader. He has been given the death sentence, not by the Mexican Army, but by the hordes of press members that descended on San Cristobal on January 1, 1994. His stock has gone from Sixty Minutes interviews to sporadic sound bytes. The press wants blood, not poetry. Even his use of the mask is losing the romanticism it once held.

Even the leadership of the EZLN wants action, and the pressure is on Marcos from all sides to perform.

Bishop Don Samuel Ruiz

Not even the bullet-proof vests that he supposedly wears can protect him from nature's aging process. However, he still invites Human Rights groups to visit Chiapas. The observers note how little food the natives have. He takes them to villages controlled by the Zapatistas, which are kept unkempt, to show the terrible conditions the Indians live in. In these villages the Indians are prisoners, not of the Mexican government, but of the EZLN, though the observers may not know that.

His break with the Pontiff means he will never be awarded a red Cardinals cap. The Nobel Prize for peace has evaded him, even after considerable pressure from his friends in Europe and the United States. Yet he is not without considerable power, and he will continue his battle for Liberation Theology as long as he holds the Bishop's position.

Persecution

Jesus said, "Remember the word that I said to you. 'A servant is not greater than his master.' If they persecuted Me, they will also persecute you." (John 15:20) The evangelicals in Chiapas can, and will even more so in days ahead, be able to identify with Paul when he wrote, "We are hard pressed on every side, yet not crushed, we are perplexed but not in despair, persecuted but not forsaken; struck down, but not destroyed, always carrying about in the body the dying of the Lord Jesus, that the life of Jesus also may be manifested in our body." (II Cor. 4:8-10)

Persecution could be ended if the evangelicals capitulated to the demands of the caciques and continued to take part in their Christopagan festivals. Of course they won't, now or ever. The main fact is that when one threatens the seat of power, persecution is not far behind.

There are several things to remember about persecution:

1. The primary catalyst for persecution in Chiapas is the believer's refusal to take part in events that are Christopagan. This threatens the seat of power, held by the caciques and the Catholic Church which collect money from the poor to finance the monthly bacchanalias. If the Indians don't have enough money for a festival, they are expected to get a loan from the caciques. Through this process, three festivals may be enough to put them in debt to the cacique for the rest of their lives.

2. There are very few churches in the world today experiencing revival where persecution has not been used by the Holy Spirit as a major catalyst for growth and purification.

3. Alexander Solzhenitsyn gave thanks for his Gulag imprisonment because it was what brought him face to face with God. Victor Frankel, a victim of the Holocaust, said "greatness comes through the crucible."

Syncretism

Basically, syncretism is the combining of pagan beliefs and rituals with Christian beliefs and rituals, which results in Christopaganism. In actual practice, it means that the Indians are allowed to incorporate pagan rituals into the Christian tradition as they see fit, as long as they both attend and financially support the church.

The terrible danger of syncretism can best be illustrated by what the missionaries in Southeast Asia called "the five foot snake." It is a bright green specimen, about ten inches long, and looks like it came right out of the Garden. It is called the "five foot snake" because when it bites and unleashes its venom, five feet is about as far as a victim can walk before the venom attacks the respiratory system and they fall down, dead.

Laos is a landlocked country. There are few cattle, fish or other sources of protein. The people are malnourished because of this lack of protein. The venom of the snake is 85 percent pure protein, which is exactly what the people need. However, the 15 percent poison makes the protein useless. There is no satisfaction in being the healthiest corpse in Laos, anymore than there is hope in Chiapas for those who are spiritually dead from the venom of a polluted gospel.

The Charismatics

In plotting the growth of Mexico's church, the Charismatic movement can't be ignored. It is the fastest growing religious group in Chiapas. They are found in the most fundamental of Evangelical and Roman Catholic churches.

At a recent conference, a Theologian at Chicago Loyola University, Jesuit Fr. John Haughey, addressed the subject from the Catholic point of view. "Charisms are to be understood, not just in the narrow sense of extraordinary manifestations, like speaking in tongues, but as gifts given 'the faithful of every rank for the sake of others' - for upbuilding the community. Most are quite ordinary and assist an individual in family, professional and community relationships, as well as in specific church activity.

According to Vatican II, the charismatic gifts which keep the church 'vital,' are distinct from the hierarchical gifts, which keep the church unified and 'orderly.' Given that distinction, how could the church make a law that would exclude a priori the freedom of the Spirit to seize some portion of the community, women for example, to minister to the community for its upbuilding. . . and we must inquire whether the serious problem we are experiencing with vocations is due to law rather than to an absence of such calls or to an unwillingness of the called to follow them. What if the call is being issued and the possibility of responding to it is not there because of law?

Because of their unpredictable nature, charisms have received uneven treatment in the history of the church and even Vatican II was quite unprepared to deal with the subject. One cardinal, Ernesto Ruffini, protested even the use of the term because he contended charisms had passed out of the church after the first years and 'are today very rare and entirely singular.'"

The National Catholic Reporter (1996) adds the following:

"Charisms proved an intriguing subject throughout the symposium. One member of a panel wondered why the Spirit is not 'a little more generous' in supplying church officeholders of mediocre talent with the charisms they need - in preaching, for example. Fr. Michael Himes, of Boston College, replied that the better question might be, 'Why are we giving office to people who don't have the charisms in the first place?'

The subject of charism was addressed in some detail by Margaret Mitchell of the McCormick Theological Seminary in Chicago in her analysis of I Corinthians. On the one hand, she said Paul seems to fully legitimate hierarchical authority, yet he stresses the 'greater honor' that is due to the seemingly inferior members of Christ's body.

Stability and order are major concerns in the church, she said, but not the only ones: Room must be made for the Holy Spirit, who often acts like 'an unruly house guest.'"

The Executive Director for Bishop Don Samuel Ruiz was asked what they would do if a revival broke out in the Evangelical church, or even in their church. "Oh it already has. Look at the Seventh Day Adventists and the Pentecostals."

The interviewer continued, "No, I mean real revival where people stop strangers on the street and ask them where they may find the real Jesus, as they are doing in Ethiopia." He replied, with some agitation, "Oh, we would not like that. We would have to do something about it."

Because evangelicals do not have a hierarchical authority, they do not have one who can act as spokesman. However, the attitude among Evangelicals, both Protestant and Roman Catholic, is that though they may disagree with the Charismatic's forms of worship and some of their theology, they admit "they are reaching more people than we are with the basics of the salvation of the people."

Five hundred Presbyterians from more than twenty congregations left their church to form Charismatic or Pentecostal churches. Those who made the move gave the following reasons for doing so:

1. Basic factions in society and unresolved tensions
2. The pattern of leadership
3. Rigidity in the system
4. Limited participation of members in worship services
5. Inadequate attention to sickness and need
6. Need for wider fellowship
7. A loss of vision

Non-charismatic congregations need to deeply consider the strengths of the Charismatic movement, not just their perceived weaknesses.

Though some evangelicals are exceedingly vocal in their

opposition to the Charismatic movement, the Charismatic's success requires that they not be ignored.

The Immigrants

Flanked by the elders of the village, the Mayan priest prays over the burned offering of copal incense, which will he believes, nourish the gods of creation. Chanting in his native language of Kanjobal to weavers, street cleaners, herbal healers and others in his parish, he kneels with robed celebrants before a wooden cross, its four points representing the full breadth of the universe. This appears to be a service in a Christopagan church in Chiapas, the center of the Mayan culture, but it is not. It is taking place in a tattered dance hall in South Central Los Angeles.

There are more than 20,000 descendants of the ancient Mayans living in Southern California. They are concentrated in three of Los Angeles' poorest districts: the South-Central, Pico-Union and Westlake neighborhoods. They are a community within a community, having brought their culture with them. A Southern California Mayan declares from his heart, "The loss of our culture will destroy our soul. . . A Mayan may be smiling on the outside, but without my culture, I am crying on the inside."

Their most influential authority is the Mayan priest, not to be confused with a Roman Catholic priest, although the meeting may be officially labeled "Catholic." The priest is known by many names, but he is essentially the traditional shaman, a village's spiritual advisor, who pre-dates the arrival of the Spanish into Mexico.

The Mayans in Los Angeles must keep their balance among three distinct worlds: their tradition-bound upbringing, the vibrant Latino spirit of contemporary Southern California, and the mainstream, predominantly English-speaking U.S. society.

Like many indigenous immigrant groups from Mexico, the Mayans tend to occupy the bottom rung of the job ladder. From the sweatshops of Los Angeles to the slaughterhouses of the

Midwest, the restaurants of Houston, and the fields of northern San Diego county, south Florida and the Pacific Northwest.

The Mayan's exodus from Mexico is largely responsible for census bureau statistics that, "for the first time, there are more Hispanic children than black children in America." They predict that by the year 2005, "Hispanics will overtake blacks as the largest minority group in the United States, and by 2050, there will be more Hispanics than all other minorities, combined."

The US government knows it is something that has to be taken into account whether you are delivering health services or education services. We could add to that, "church services."

The Lord's words, "Go into the world and make disciples," appears to include the implication, "and if you don't go to them, I will bring them to you." Such may well be the case in Los Angeles today. A recent Los Angeles Times headline read: "L.A.'s Latino immigrants are remaking the city's spiritual landscape with . . . An Evangelical Revival."

The article's insightful author, Ruben Martinez, points out, "There are some 1,000 Latino Protestant churches in the city of Los Angeles alone, the majority of which are evangelical. There are thousands more throughout the Southwest. Even within the Catholic Church, the Pentecostal influence is felt. The number of 'charismatic' churches, congregations that want to remain within the Catholic flock, but seek the kind of spiritual pyrotechnics of the evangelicals, is on the rise." Martinez adds," This movement is also powered to a great extent by Latinos. . . Pentecostalism is the religion of our times. It has the right tone (apocalyptic), the right rhythm (fast), the right philosophy (communitarianism as a salve for urban fragmentation and paranoia). You might say Pentecostalism is the MTV of religions."

Whatever it is called, it certainly echoes another great event in Los Angeles history, which took place on April 9, 1906, in a wood-frame house in the area known today as Pico-Union. The Holy Spirit came down as it did at Pentecost. No one cared that the pastor, Rev. William Seymour, was African American, and that the congregation was made up of whites, Mexicans and blacks. What they had in common was that they were all of modest means, they were the "forgotten and disenfranchised," whom mainline churches had gradually, but ultimately, neglected. It has been called the Azusa Street Revival.

Martinez writes: "Nearly a century later, on the cusp of the millennium, and with not a little millennialism in the air, Los Angeles is on its way to fulfilling the promise of Azusa Street." That revival literally spread around the world, and is still being felt today."

Martinez concludes: "Today, Pentecostalism is a symbol of the new Los Angeles. The majority of the faithful are Latino, about evenly split between immigrants and their native-born children. Not just Los Angeles, but the entire Southern California "landscape is being remade by storefront churches, housed almost exclusively in older buildings, some of which were on the verge of collapse before the arrival of the spiritual revolutionaries." There is no rebellion here, just good old spiritual revolutionaries.

Hope

The native Chiapans, whose hope has been incessantly crushed still long for and hope that someone, somewhere, will right four and a half centuries of injustice.

We weep with them, realizing that hope is a necessary part of our nature. One writer has written; "We sleep in hope of rest. We wake in hope of day. We work in hope of tomorrow. We marry in hope of companionship. We have children in hope of joy. We run the race in hope of victory. We fight wars in hope of freedom. We bear the darkness in hope of light. We live in hope of eternity."

But how long can a people continue to exist on hope alone, if their rest is on a mat on a dirt floor in a one room shack? If they wake up each day finding nothing has changed? If they cry out for strength day after day after day, only to find none? The cry is a sad litany of an oppressed people, living across the border from men and women whose hope is in the stock market, in accumulating wealth, in IRAs and new cars. Can we ever understand that these people, who shed real tears just like us, cling to hope, like all of us, as motivation for some purposeful action?

Like millions before them, the Indians of Chiapas realize that where there is no hope, there is no reason to live. An experiment was done with mice at the University of North Carolina, where each was placed in a container half full of water. One container was sealed, and when the creature realized there was no hope of escape, gave up swimming and drowned in three minutes. The second container was not sealed, leaving the possibility of escape and survival. That mouse swam for thirty-six hours.

How tired the arms of the Chiapans must be getting. At what point will they stop swimming, give up and sink to the bottom? Our Indian brothers and sisters know from personal experience, their hearts, minds and bodies, ready to simply collapse in tired, grief-stricken humanity, that the absence of hope is the essence of despair.

A prisoner of the in North Vietnam said of his fellow aviators in a prison camp in Hanoi, that a man was told by the Viet Cong that he would be released in a week. He was not released, but a new date was set. After several release dates passed without his release, he lost hope. In a short time, he was found in a fetal position, naked, in the farthest corner of his cell, dead.

Eric Fromm wrote, "If a person has given up hope, he has entered the gates of hell, whether he knows it or not, and has left behind him his own humanity."

How many of the Indians in Chiapas have given up hope? How many times must they place their hope in what turns out to be a cruel maneuver to make someone else rich at their expense? More importantly, how can hope be restored? The last thing that dies in a person is hope. Revolutions and rebellions begin because it is the nature of this world to try to starve out hope. It's been almost 500 years now for the Indians of Chiapas. How much longer can they swim?

Einstein concluded that the greatest question facing humankind is whether the universe is friendly or hostile. The Indian's scars, and bent, cross-bearing backs give the dark answer.

When this question is brought to the Word of God, there is light. In its creation, the universe is friendly. In its fall, it is hostile to the core. The landowners, the caciques, the politicians, the members of the rebel groups, these will all lose their hope as well one day when they come to the end of the things upon which their hope is built.

In the experiment with the mice, the first died from lack of hope, but the second died for lack of help. Who will help the helpless? It will not be a truncated Gospel, a rag-tag army, a Bishop on a donkey, a religion that encompasses half-truths and half-lies, or a rebel poet.

Where is hope to be found, and on what help can that hope be based? To find the answer, we must grasp the scarlet thread that runs through all of Chiapas' long history. While the Hebrew nation was learning about God's plan to reach down and redeem man, the forefathers of today's Chiapans were crossing the Bering Straits and moving down the west coast of what is now the United States, eventually arriving in Mexico. They brought with them their understanding of God, an understanding based on truth, but already distorted.

The history of Chiapas is the story of a people seeking redemption and forgiveness, standing on their tip toes, crawling to the high places, attempting to touch the finger of God. In an orgy of ignorance, the Mayans and others sacrificed hundreds of thousands of victims. When the Spanish conquistadors arrived they continued the practice, sacrificing ten million natives to "free" them from their pagan ways. Under the rule of the Mayans, there was blood on the sacred altar, the blood of the people. With colonization, there was blood on the sword.

The Mayans and their forefathers were very religious. However, religion and Christianity are as different as night and day. Religion is mankind's attempt to reach up to God. Christianity, on the other hand, is God's reaching down to touch man.

There is a famous painting by Michelangelo in Rome's Sistine Chapel, depicting the God of heaven reaching out with his fingertip to touch the outstretched hand of man - God giving His life to man. God not only gave His life to man that He had made in His image. He also became a man, in order to give up His lifeblood for mankind. This was the only sacrifice that could bring about fallen man's redemption.

Blood is life. The Indians understood this, just as the Hebrews were taught, "The life of the flesh is in the blood."2

In modern Euro-American culture, it is difficult for us to understand the significance of blood. The very word brings to mind pain, disease, and disgust. However, blood is life. Chiapans have a less difficult time understanding the importance of the blood, and are embracing the good news that in Christ's blood is hope for their redemption.

The people God chose to demonstrate the truth about His character learned about the significance of blood when He was about to free them from Egyptian oppression. He explained the supernatural purpose of blood on the occasion of a night that came to be known as the Passover. He said, "Now I will pass through the land of Egypt on that night and will strike all the first born in the land of Egypt, both men and beast, and against all the gods of Egypt I will execute judgment. I am the Lord. Now the blood shall be a sign: and they shall take some of the blood from the sacrificial lamb and put it on the two doorposts and on the lintel of the house where they eat of the lamb. . . Now the blood shall be a sign for you and the plagues shall not destroy you when I strike the land of Egypt."3

Later, God gave these words of assurance to his people that

the Chiapans so desperately want to hear for themselves: "I have seen the afflictions of my people and have heard their cry and so have come to liberate them."

The unfolding revelation of the necessity of a blood sacrifice began in Exodus at the Passover, and was completed at Calvary when Jesus cried out, "It is finished!" Revelation, the final book in the Bible, tells of the defeat of the great deceiver, God's enemy, who called for the loathsome human sacrifices. "In her was found the blood of prophets and of saints and of all who have been slain on the earth." But there will be a final triumph when the Lamb of God comes for all those who believe in His finished sacrifice. He will arrive with eyes aflame with righteousness. "He is clothed with a robe dipped in blood and His name is called The Word of God. . . and on his robe. . . He has a name written, 'King of Kings and Lord of Lords.'" This is the hoped for and assured future, but today, the people are still carrying a heavy cross of rebellion, syncretism and persecution.

But now, at last, the Chiapans have been given a sword meant for good, the Sword of the Lord, the Holy Word of God in their own native tongue. It is for the Chiapans now to feed on the Word, translated for them by the missionaries. The good news of Ephesians 1:7 is now available for the taking: "In Him we have redemption through the blood, the forgiveness of sins, according to the riches of His grace." Hebrews 9:1 seals the promise that redemption and freedom have been purchased, "not with the blood of goats and calves" - or humans, chickens or cats - "but with His own blood He entered the most high place once and for all to judge the quick and the dead."

The scarlet thread of blood, that reaches so far back with its accumulated misunderstandings and false teachings, must be cleansed and purified by the truth found in God's Word about Jesus Christ and His blood sacrifice. "For it pleased the Father that in Him all the fullness should dwell, and by Him to reconcile all things to Himself, whether things on earth or things in heaven, having made peace..." Not through the Zapatistas, the

Bishop, the caciques, or Marcos. There can be peace, but only through the blood of His cross.

In Jesus' instruction to "eat of his flesh and drink his blood" Christ meant that all who believe, even the people of Chiapas, need to feed their hearts and souls and minds on Him, and to allow Him to give them abundant new life, through His life and His blood, until they are filled with the life of Jesus Christ.

Today, deep in the darkness of Chiapas, this message is being received among both Evangelicals and Catholics. An effective blood sacrifice has been discovered, a complete and finished sacrifice that makes any continued sacrifices worthless. It is the blood of the Creator God's Son. It is powerful enough to satisfy eternity's requirements. The blood of Jesus Christ is filling veins that ran dry with fear, cleansing hearts that were once filled with hate, liberating spirits that were once captive to despair. The weariness of poverty and the pain of injustice still remain, but no fear, no superstition, no depression, and no desperation can quench the power of the blood of Jesus Christ in their lives.

More and more, the Indians of Chiapas are realizing that He is Jehovah-Rafa, the God who Heals, who has come to offer the blood of life to every Indian in Chiapas, to free them from their sins. The Good News is spreading like wildfire.

Christ is their hope, but in their present sufferings they must remember that Jesus sweat drops of blood in Gethsemane before giving His blood at Calvary. God always meets His children at their point of submission, at their Gethsemane, at their reaching up to Him. There are no short cuts to Pentecost, but no one is left to make the journey alone. The song writer, G.A. Young put it well:

Though sorrows befall us, and Satan oppose,
God leads His dear children along;
Through grace we can conquer, defeat all our foes,

God leads His dear children along.

Some through the water, some through the flood,

Some through the fire, but all through the blood;

Some through great sorrow, but God gives a song,

In the night season and all the day long.[4]

   Be praying for the believers in Chiapas, and listening for all of them - Evangelical, Catholic and Charismatic - to join together with believers everywhere to sing:

What can wash away my sin? Nothing but the blood of Jesus!

What can make me whole again? Nothing but the blood of Jesus!

Oh, precious is the flow that makes me white as snow,

No other fount I know,

NOTHING BUT THE BLOOD OF JESUS![5]

Epilogue: The Gathering in the Zocalo (town square)
Taken from an onlooker's journal March 21, 1998

In the zocalo of San Cristobal, shoe shine boys and corn cob vendors drift between the dusty park benches and the trees. Friday ends with a sigh, as barefoot and ragged children move about in the shadows of the cathedral which guards one end of the square. Behind the statehouse on the zocalo's other border, the discordant notes of an amateur band and a gathering crowd invite a curious audience. As spontaneous as the music may sound, the activity behind the zocalo is not an impulse, like most of the other colorful entertainment in the square on weekend evenings. Tonight is the rally.

Time has passed since the attack. The wounds on Pasquala's body are healing in their own crude fashion, but the scars on her soul are more difficult to cover. Many a dark night she lies awake, recalling the whisper of her sisters' laughter from the waiting world beyond, longing to speak with them once again. Yet every tremulous nightmare of the past is bathed in the soothing life and presence of Jehovah-Rafa.

I couldn't keep the lump from my throat or the tear from my eye, I was standing on the edge of something I recognized, but was sure I couldn't understand. It was the moment. . . the moment where the lens focused, if just for an instant, in all of this jumbled history. In that instant, I saw the hope, the justice, the true liberation, the liberation of the heart.

Pasquala slips through a woven fabric of bodies around the fragile plywood stage, carried by the harmonies of an eternal song of praise to Jesu Cristo, the God who heals. Dancers in white dresses spin through the mix of bodies with silver tambourines, laughing like Miriam at the exodus. Having been freed from despair's captivity, two thousand unshackled hands wave wisps of white paper as their victory banner to the heavens. A man takes the microphone and begins to pray...

Are they any less poor? Do they have shoes to cover the bare, callused skin of their feet, cracked as the tile beneath them? The child with eyes alive and burning, gripping her mother's tiny hand and ducking into the coarse folds of her wool skirt. . . is she any less hungry, does she have any more tortillas than before?

No.

Yet they smile. Their toughened feet shuffle on the stones like the murmur of dry cornstalks in a summer breeze. An infant, cradled in the bright scarf around her mother's neck, turns uplifted face and drinks life itself. Her Mother too is looking up, filling her tired soul with the life and presence of her Savior.

"El Senor esta aqui" (the Father is here) they cheer, hands clamoring skyward, seeking the bread of life. From the balcony some look on, with spiritual hunger pangs too strong to ignore. Could freedom be here, without a gun, without a priest, without a cost?

The dancers swing their tambourines, a spinning glow in the twilight. The crowd sings in joyful unison, praising their Lord and Savior.

I have seen the answer, and He is here among them.

On the torn bricks of the village square, one can hear the shuffle of a Savior's feet.

Introduction
1. Genesis 3:21; 4:3-5; 9:4
2. II Chronicles 28:3; Ezekiel 16:20-21
3. Habakkuk

Chapter One
Photo: Young Indian Vendor, San Cristobal, October 1998
1. The Ancient Kingdoms of Mexico, Nigel Davies, Penguin, 1986
2. Meeting God in Holy Places, F. LaGard Smith, Harvest House Pub.
3. Mestizos: When the Aztecs were conquered by the Spaniards, the two groups intermarried. From these marriages came the dominating influence in Mexico today, the mestizos, sometimes called "The Mexico City Man."
4. Yajval Balamil: Tzotzil name for the earth lord, who lives under the surface of the earth and is the ruler and sender of clouds, wind, rain and everything that is produced on earth.

Chapter Two
Photo: Church Remnants, Outskirts of San Juan Chamula, November 1996
1. It is strongly recommended that those who wish to further pursue this subject read The Devastation of the Indies: a Brief Account, by Bartalome de las Casas, John Hopkins Press.
2. The authors are grateful to Dr. Henry Aulie for giving them permission to quote extensively from his doctoral dissertation for Fuller Theological Seminary, School of World Missions. Dr. Aulie spent most of his adult life in Chiapas, Mexico as a missionary/Bible translator. Each time Dr. Aulie is mentioned, it will refer to The Christian Movement Among the Chols of Mexico With Special Reference To Problems Of Second Generation

Christianity, copyright May 1, 1979 and available from University Microfilms International, 300 N. Zeeb Rd., Ann Arbor, MI 48106

3. The English American - His Travail By Sea And Land: 1648 Also published under the title, New Survey Of The West-Indies London - R. Cotes and quoted in Dr. Aulie's dissertation

4. Ximenez, Fray Francisco, Historia de la Provincia de San Vicente de Chiapa y Guatemala, quoted from Dr. Aulie's dissertation

Chapter Three

Photo: Evangelical Refugees, Settlement of Nuevo Jerusalem, Ocosingo, November 1996

Chapter Four

Photo: Sub-Comandante Marcos, Government Sponsored Peace Talks, San Cristobal, November 1996

1. Note: for a complete report on the 1994 Rebellion, one must read Pulitzer Prize winner, Andres Oppenheimer's BORDERING ON CHAOS: Guerrillas, Stockbrokers, Politicians, and Mexico's Road to Prosperity. Little, Brown, and Co. 1996.

2. Trvialization of God, Donald W. McCulloch, NavPress

Chapter Five

Photo: Church Members, Settlement of Nuevo Jerusalem, Ocosingo, November 1996

1. For the complete story of these pioneers, one should read: The Good Seed, Marianna Slocum and Grace Watkins, Promise Pub., 1988

2. Matthew 10:34

3. John 16:33

4. John 3:19-20

Chapter Six

Photo: Indian Girl with Infant, San Juan Chamula, November 1996

1. Open Doors Newsbrief, October 1996
2. A Theology of War, Steven A. Engel, Unpublished, 1996
3. Christ and Crisis, Charles Malik, Wm. B. Erdmans Pub. Co., 1962

Conclusion

1. The Mexican Shock, Jorge Castaneda, New Press, NY, 1995
2. Leviticus 17:11
3. Exodus 12
4. God Lead Us Along, G.A. Young, Nazarene Pub., 1931
5. Nothing But the Blood, Robert Lowry, public domain

Cover Photo: Cesar L. Laure